THE
HOPE
CHALLENGE
Devotional

Xulon Press
2301 Lucien Way #415
Maitland, FL 32751
407.339.4217
www.xulonpress.com

Unless otherwise indicated, Scripture quotations taken from the English Standard Version (ESV). Copyright © 2001 by Crossway, a publishing ministry of Good News Publishers. Used by permission. All rights reserved.

Paperback ISBN-13: 978-1-6628-2596-5
Ebook ISBN-13: 978-1-6628-2597-2

For Zarat

Acknowledgements

Emily A. -You are a Rockstar. Thank you
for taking the gibberish that I write and
making it into something worth sharing.

Pete & Geri -Thank you for exposing me
to exploring the Icebergs of grief and loss.

Brian and Amy -I am grateful that you loved me
through my dark season and never wavered.

Aaron and Tracy – Thank you for
encouraging me as this poured out.

The Vertical Family – I am honored to know you and
to have been able to do life alongside you while going
through the toughest season of my life.
You are the best!

I love you all and you make me better.

Preface

Life can be hard, even for Jesus followers. We can fully submit our lives to Christ and still face disease, loss, sadness, disappointment, and hopelessness. Many of our Biblical heroes encountered hardships that almost overwhelmed them. We see their obstacles in retrospect as we read the scriptures, and we usually know that everything is going to end well. That was not true for them; their stories were still being written and could have ended less than favorably. Most of the time what they knew was their God existed and that He had their lives safely in His hands. Their future was not fully in their control as they had to hope in God for their success and safety. God in His sovereignty took care of them, and He will take care of you.

God is good, but everything He allows in our lives doesn't always feel good. We are in fact in a world where jobs are lost, sickness in rampant, and depression looms heavy. As long as we are alive, we will have to endure trials that will hopefully grow our faith. Instead of running from our struggles and our emotions connected to them, we should prepare ourselves for the inevitable. To find hope in God is a great gift, and it should keep us moving forward no matter our circumstances. Some key topics addressed are...

- Living with Gratitude
- Handling Stress
- Overcoming Feelings of Condemnation
- Embracing Your Identity in Christ
- Enlarging Your Perspective
- Processing Betrayal & Disappointment
- Dealing with Anxiety

This devotional is designed with a challenge to help you take steps toward the God of Hope. It will prayerfully allow you to process through the Bible with your thoughts and feeling rather than yielding to the temptation to use your thoughts and feeling to process the Bible! Our emotions can lie to us, so we must see them in the light of the scriptures. The best way to walk through this journey is with a friend(s) who will remind you of who you are and whose you are when you are facing these dark seasons of the soul that will come. Going through this book with others should give you some needed feedback and insight that can be elusive during difficult times.

Commit to completing the challenges! Some will be very relevant to your current situation while others may seem like mere task to be accomplished. Others will only make sense upon their completion yet may transform your perspective for the better. The only way to know how God might speak to you is to do it. Trust

God to guide you through the process and rely on Him to give you the hope you need.

God Bless you on this Journey,

1
GRATITUDE

Gratitude lifts and elevates the soul. Believers and unbelievers alike benefit from practicing gratefulness. It is probably because being grateful forces one's eyes off oneself and onto God's goodness. It's hard to exist in disappointment and gratitude at the same time.

Pain of any kind tends to be selfish. We can see this selfishness most naturally in the physical presentation of pain. If a person is experiencing physical pain, all of their attention and focus goes to the ache. Every moment is harder as it is, in part defined by the discomfort. It's very difficult for a person to block out their hurt to focus on anything else. Elite athletes are often defined by how they manage their injuries and the agony associated with it. Emotional disappointment, sadness, and trauma can be tremendously uncomfortable, but because these do not immediately appear in one's body, they can go unseen. We only start to recognize pain in a person's actions over time. Too often someone gets labeled difficult, mean, or selfish when the problem is that they are carrying an emotional injury.

No one is labeling you today, but it would serve you well to discover the root of the discomfort.

> *"Therefore, let us be grateful for receiving a kingdom that cannot be shaken, and thus let us offer to God acceptable worship, with reverence and awe, for our God is a consuming fire." Hebrews 12:28-29*

This scripture encourages us to be grateful for receiving a gift from God that can't be shaken: His Kingdom! Jesus fought for you on His cross, to induct you into that very same Kingdom. You may feel shaken by your current reality, but God is not. You are a part of something so much bigger than you. Our God who is a powerful, consuming fire has and will continue to fight for you. Whether you feel like it or not, the Bible tells us to be grateful. It can take great effort on your part, but it is necessary for you to have a healthy life.

Challenge: Write a list of God's gifts to you—His divine attributes that have been lovingly bestowed on you; His love, His Kingdom, His kindness; and so on. This can help you to turn your eyes to our glorious God and His goodness and take your eyes off of your struggles.

2
Blessed

When enduring a dark season of the soul, it's hard to rejoice! It is hard to pray. Being thankful is often the farthest thing from your mind. What usually grips a person in these dark moments is despair. Not that despair is desired or wished for; it is simply a part of a hard season. Paul was encouraging the church at Thessalonica when he said,

"Rejoice always, pray without ceasing, give thanks in all circumstances; for this is the will of God in Christ Jesus for you." 1 Thessalonians 5:16-18

It is the will of God that you rejoice, which means to be glad. It may seem crazy to tell someone who is sad to simply be glad, but it helps to know that God desires that for you. He is invested in your gladness. This doesn't mean that you won't have unpleasant moments, but that God's plan for your life includes gladness. The joy expressed here is not temporary, it emanates from knowing who God is and who you are in Him. Joy is not determined by how we feel.

To pray without ceasing sounds like an unrealistic task. When would you sleep? This does not mean continuously, but from moment to moment. It only makes sense to take your cries, concerns, and complaints to God. It is always a good thing. He longs to hear about the worries that burden you. You have a Heavenly Father who cares about what you care about. He may not feel the same way you do about those issues, but He cares that you care. This should give you hope.

We are told to give thanks in all circumstances. This might seem impossible. All circumstances, really? Yes, even that! Whatever you are going through, God knows the end from the beginning. He knew exactly what you would face, and He wants you to give thanks—not for the hard times, but in the hard times. Believers are expected to thank God even when everything in life is telling them to give up. In your worst moments, you can find something to rejoice over, pray for, and give thanks about.

Challenge: Today, write a list of things for which you are thankful. Start with the simple: life, health, and strength for whatever condition they might be experiencing. Next, look to the practical: a home, a job, a family, friends, etc. Then move on to the intangible: for example, love and new opportunities. You may be surprised to discover you are more blessed than you realize.

3

GARMENT OF PRAISE

L ife is interesting; often the very thing we need is the very last thing we want. When your hope is low, the last thing you want to do is praise God. But that is the very thing you need. We want to praise when we feel like it, not when we don't. So much of the Christian life is exactly that way. When repentance is needed, we want to run and hide like Adam and Eve. Not the healthiest choice. We need light, but we run to darkness. That is the human condition, and followers of Jesus are bad at this too.

Isaiah speaks prophetically of the Messiah, which Jesus Himself confirms at the beginning of His ministry (Luke 4:17-19). Let us look to the original writing to extract our lesson for today.

The Spirit of the Lord God is upon me, because the Lord has anointed me to bring good news to the poor; he has sent me to bind up the brokenhearted, to proclaim liberty to the captives, and the opening of the prison to those who are bound; to proclaim the year of the Lord's favor, and the day of vengeance of our God; to comfort all who mourn; to grant to those who mourn in Zion— to give them a beautiful headdress instead of ashes, the oil of gladness instead of mourning, the garment of praise instead of a faint spirit; that they may be called oaks of righteousness, the planting of the Lord, that he may be glorified. Isaiah 61:1-3

God's sovereign Spirit anointed Him for the purpose changing the trajectories of people's lives. The poor would be seen and given good news. The brokenhearted would be comforted and healed. This may make no sense to someone whose heart has never been broken, but those who have experienced deep heartache are desperate for this kind of comfort and healing. Those who are imprisoned would find freedom and new life in Him. We have enough additional scripture to know that this is not just a message for those who are physically bound, but also those who experience mental and emotional bondage. All this is happening because the Lord would be coming! Those of us that are in perpetual mourning would find comfort, and we would no longer have to wear the look of one who has lost deeply.

Then we get one last, curious exchange. We get a garment of praise instead of the spirit so heavy that it makes us feel faint. So, Jesus gave us all of these things to help those of us in need. He is not withholding these things from His people; they are available now. Pay particular attention to the garment that we get to wear: praise! We don't often see praise as a garment. To get rid of heaviness, we need praise, even though we don't always want to praise when we feel heavy. We need to put that on and wear it to chase away the fainting that wants to weigh us down. God already gave it to you—will you put it on?

Challenge: Praise God today, out loud. Sing songs that speak of His goodness and love. Search the internet for songs that lift you and remind you that God loves and sees you. It doesn't matter how you sound to others. God gave you that gift, and He loves to hear you sing to Him.

4

CHANGE YOUR THINKING

Our minds are more powerful than we often believe. How a person thinks affects how they live. If you want to live a better life, begin to see things the way God sees them. We can let our thoughts run away with us, then let those same thoughts condemn us on the journey. We have to learn to arrest wayward thoughts in order to maintain our hold on reality. We must hold not only the reality of this broken world, but also that of the real and greater Kingdom that God has called us to experience in this life in preparation for the next.

The Apostle Paul stresses this point in his second letter to the church at Corinth. He defends his ministry and admonishes the believers to live differently than the culture in which they find themselves. He points out that believers are at war with this world's way of functioning. This world's thinking is not the mindset Jesus intends for His disciples.

"For the weapons of our warfare are not of the flesh but have divine power to destroy strongholds. We destroy arguments and every lofty opinion raised against the knowledge of God, and take every thought captive to obey Christ, being ready to punish every disobedience, when your obedience is complete." 2 Corinthians 10:4-6

We have to fight against the enemy within. Sometimes we are our greatest opposition. Far too often, we can get in our own way. Fear, stress, and worry can all create hopelessness. We all must first win the battle in our own minds! That is where internal struggle beats us. You want to defeat your enemy? It starts with changing how you think! Arrest those thoughts with the truth of God's Word. The best way to fight a lie, even one told you by your own brain, is with God's unfiltered truth.

That was Jesus' approach as He faced the devil and was tempted (Matthew 4). The world uses logic, reasoning, and personal feelings to measure right and wrong. These have to take a backseat to the Word of God. For followers of Jesus, the Bible is our ultimate gauge for truth.

Challenge: Take some time to research a scripture or two that speak to your specific challenges. If you are wrestling with faith, find scripture that encourages your faith. If your greatest struggle is sadness, find something that speaks of joy. Take responsibility for your biblical growth in an effort to renew your mind.

5
PRAYER EXCHANGE

Everyone wants to be heard. People go through their lives hoping to find someone to understand and identify with their thoughts, opinions, and feelings. They don't necessarily need to be told they are right, but to simply know that someone cares enough to hear their perspectives and inner thoughts—what a gift. That is why people spend time and money on professionals to listen—it's that important. To be heard, deeply heard, soothes the soul.

Whether we go to a spouse, parent, sibling, best friend, or a mental health professional, we need to have someone with whom we can speak freely. A trusted person will allow enough space to let their loved one process with little to no judgment. It is a good practice to say, "I need to vent. I don't want advice. I just need to share what I am thinking out loud." This statement creates space for a person to process verbally what is going on internally.

The great news is that your first audience is the best audience. God wants to hear your prayers! Jesus taught His disciples to pray.

"Pray then like this: 'Our Father in heaven, hallowed be your name. Your kingdom come, your will be done, on earth as it is in heaven. Give us this day our daily bread, and forgive us our debts, as we also have forgiven our debtors. And lead us not into temptation, but deliver us from evil.'" Matthew 6:9-13

God is our Father, and He cares about the issues of our hearts. We can tell him how sorry we are for letting Him down (which we all do at some point), and He also wants to hear about our worries and fears. It is a blessing to have people willing to listen to our hearts cry, but there is nothing better than knowing that God Himself wants to hear our prayers. We can say whatever is needed and know with confidence that He is big enough to handle it.

The problem we have with prayer is that most people don't know what the word means, so we miss all its beauty. The root word in the original language is *Proseuchomai*—to interact with the Lord by switching human wishes or ideas for His wishes as He imparts faith. Prayer is an exchange. That is the difference between talking to people and talking to God. God cannot only change our situations; He changes our hearts in the process. So, we can even take Him our wrongs, and He makes them right. The power of prayer is in this exchange. It is processing, and it is also transforming.

Challenge: Today take some intentional time to pray. Set aside at least 10-15 minutes for this purpose. Pray about the things that worry or scare you, the issues in your heart that you are nervous to voice to another person. Tell Him about the things that excite and inspire you. He wants to hear them. Ask Him to guide you to the best ways of both thinking and being. Trust your Heavenly Father to hear and respond in the way He deems best.

6
LOOK TO THE HILLS

Where do you go when you don't know where to go? This question may seem challenging to some, but the answer is rather easy: go to God. Why would that not be the automatic answer? Life, at least in the West, is about self-determination. You are responsible for your own results. Success is actually a complex combination of competence, networking, fate, education, etc. But, people love to tout the praises of the "self-made" person. All it takes is a series of unfortunate events to remind us that we can control very little in this life. So, what's the solution ...

"I lift up my eyes to the hills. From where does my help come? My help comes from the Lord, who made heaven and earth. Psalm 121:1-2

If you are unsure where to look, this Psalm gives you the perfect place. Look up to the source of all things. The problem with looking up is that we don't know what we will get back. At least with our own efforts we can have an expected result; with God, you don't know what He will choose to do. You may be asking Him for more money, and He may give you challenges that increase your endurance. You may look to Him for direction, and He may add to your peace. He is sovereign and knows what you need even if it is not what you want.

We all need to learn how to trust Him with the results. You are expected to give God your best efforts. When you have a task ahead of you, pursue excellence—it's a good thing. Then, rely on God for the result. Give God your best and trust Him with the rest! Remember you are not ultimately responsible for any more than your greatest effort. Learn all that you can, develop your skills, but leave the outcome in His hands.

Challenge: Confess to God every area in which you have failed to rely on Him. Maybe it's your job, your family, or how you manage your finances—those places where you have relied on yourself alone. Ask Him to help you learn to depend on Him rather than on human efforts.

7

OVERWHELMED

S ometimes life can be overwhelming! There can be so much coming at you at one time that it produces our innate fight or flight response. Even worse than that, many seem to have the much less explored freeze response too. Like a deer captivated by headlights, we can be stuck between the first two responses when impending danger comes closer and closer. It doesn't matter which of these things you may be experiencing at this particular time, what matters is that in these moments our faith misfires. Instinct is all we feel like we have. Some people thrive in these moments while others seem to wilt. The key is to learn how to thrive.

Elisha was an Old Testament prophet and the protégé of Elijah. Both were powerful voices of challenge to the northern kingdom of Israel and the surrounding area. Elisha was so influential that it was said of him that God tells Elisha what's going on in the king's bedroom. When the king heard this, he intended to kill

Elisha. This does not create fear for the prophet, but the servant was scared.

He was probably a new servant for Elisha. The last one was cursed with leprosy for trying to manipulate a financial blessing for himself in God's name. This is never a good idea! It's not hard to imagine that this new servant was nervous and probably a little scared. Well, after hearing that Elisha was in the city of Dothan, the king sent a great army to surround the entire city.

"When the servant of the man of God rose early in the morning and went out, behold, an army with horses and chariots was all around the city. And the servant said, "Alas, my master! What shall we do?" He said, "Do not be afraid, for those who are with us are more than those who are with them." Then Elisha prayed and said, "O Lord, please open his eyes that he may see." So the Lord opened the eyes of the young man, and he saw, and behold, the mountain was full of horses and chariots of fire all around Elisha." 2 Kings 6:16-17

They were literally overwhelmed by the numbers surrounding them. The servant was not wrong; his fear was justified based on his perspective. If they were going to fight their way out, they faced insurmountable odds against an entire trained army. Can you identify with that feeling? The servant was overwhelmed, just like you are sometimes. It benefited no one to ignore the obvious opposition.

Elisha, though, had a much different point of view. He saw that God had surrounded the enemy that was surrounding them! You may not realize it, but the same thing is true of you. God has you covered, even if you can't see it! He is bigger and greater than whatever challenge you are facing. When we see things from that perspective, we can rest in the thought that we will be fine. God has us.

Challenge: Elisha prayed for his servant's perspective, so we will pray for ours. Pray this simple prayer three times today:

My Father in Heaven, please open my eyes, so that I might see things from Your perspective rather than mine. Help me to rest in the thought that the things overwhelming me are not overwhelming You. You are bigger than all my challenges and fears.

In Jesus' Name, Amen.

8
Hope in God

Why are you cast down, O my soul,
and why are you in turmoil within me?
Hope in God; for I shall again praise him,
my salvation and my God. Psalm 43:5

This writer knows what it's like to struggle with one's emotions. The sorrow in his tone is all too familiar. Many people have no idea that the Bible has such deep sadness. Some assume that with God on your side everything should be happy and easy, but that is not reality. The truth is that even the most "spiritual" people can wrestle with great melancholy.

The honesty present in this psalm should give those challenged in their minds hope. You are not the only one! It is almost as if there is a grand collective of denial in our current culture. Everyone puts on a happy face and pretends as if we are fine. The fact is most people have several of these tough emotional seasons in a lifetime. For an unfortunate few, this is a lifetime's journey that has to be engaged every day in some way.

Our challenge is that these feelings come from a variety of places and reveal themselves in a variety of ways. There are people who enter a low place via trauma and others through loss. Any life transition can trigger a bout of the proverbial blues. Since this is so normal, you should not allow yourself to feel shame. If a psalmist, who wrote biblical truth, can feel what you are feeling, then know that God not only knows what you are experiencing; He is for you in spite of what you are going through. That is why we can appreciate the tone of hopefulness at the end of the psalm, "I will praise Him again," even if we struggle to feel hopeful now.

Challenge: The question the psalmist asked was, Why? Today consider the issues that most easily dishearten you. This is not an exploration of how you feel about those matters, but rather an identification of the causes. Write them down to give them the attention they require.

9
LOVE GIVES

*"For God so loved the world, that he gave his only Son,
that whoever believes in him should not perish but
have eternal life. For God did not send his Son into
the world to condemn the world, but in order that the
world might be saved through him."*
John 3:16-17

This is undoubtedly one of the most known and quoted scriptures in the Bible. God loves the world, and you are in it! We could start there and it would be enough. The God of the universe, who created all things, sees you in all your human brokenness and still loves you. How amazing is that thought?

This is not the same as the earthly love we know. In our world, we use the term *love* too frequently and too loosely. A person may say, "I love my child" and "I love pizza" in the very next moment. Those are not nearly the same sentiment. This love that God has for us is

His perfect and unrelenting love. It is a love that can't be earned but is given freely without reserve. The proof of this is what He did with this love: He gave. He gave us Jesus as a substitutionary atonement for our sin. He loved so much that He was moved into action to pay our debt, which we could never pay on our own.

He didn't want us to have to face the penalty that our sin required. Through His love, we get to embrace the forgiveness provided in Jesus' death on the cross. This is the basis for the Christian faith. This is the message that saves all to the glory of God. God is so good and loving that He eradicates our faults. This is good news.

God loved, so He gave! His followers are supposed to follow His example of generosity. One of the most challenging things to do when you are going through a hard time is to love others well. If we love, we should give also. This allows us to not only embrace the Gospel, but to put it in action.

Challenge: Consider one person in your life that you love, and you know loves you. It could be a parent, spouse, child, or a true friend. Today, find a way to express to them how much they mean to you. It could be by preparing a meal, spending time doing something they enjoy, or even something as simple as writing a kind note. Be careful not to make this moment about you. This is your moment to make it about them.

10
Not Condemned

W e are often our own worst critics. We have the
ability to see our faults, flaws, and failures and
focus so intently on them that we see no opportunity
for forgiveness. We live in our heads and have firsthand
knowledge of our own inadequacy. Add in relationships where other people start to pile on disappointment for our mistakes, and it can be a prescription for
poor self-image.

The one person who knows more of your weaknesses is
God. Being omniscient, of course, He sees where you
don't measure up and is waiting to judge you, right?
Wrong! We often view God as a mean taskmaster who
can't wait to discipline us for the mistakes we make.
This is far from true. The entire point of Jesus going to
the cross was to create distance between you and God's
wrath. He loves you and has always wanted you free
from the penalty of your faults.

"There is therefore now no condemnation for those who are in Christ Jesus."
Romans 8:1

Most of the previous chapter in Romans is about the Apostle Paul and how he can't keep from stumbling in sin. If that was where the letter had ended, things would have been quite bleak, but thank God it's not. Paul was an Apostle, and we got a glimpse into his struggle with depravity. King David stole a friend's wife and killed him. Elijah, after a great victory, ran away scared. Peter denied Jesus within earshot of his friend, and God still used Peter to bring people to the faith. If these "spiritual giants" can be so flawed yet loved and used by God, there is so much hope for you.

Whatever our difficulties in doing the right things, God is not condemning those who have accepted Jesus as their life and reward. Jesus was in fact condemned on our behalf, so we did not have to be, and this pleased our Heavenly Father! Yes, you may fail at times; you may disappoint yourself. But God is still on your side and looking for you to embrace His forgiveness and try again.

Challenge: Memorize Romans 8:1, so that the next time you are tempted to condemn yourself or to think that God is condemning you, this scripture will help you recalibrate.

11

LIFE IS MEANT TO BE LIVED

Sometimes it is important to drop the "F" word ... FUN! This elusive yet necessary concept should be active and constant in your life. When enduring hard seasons, we can all too quickly become serious, exclusively. It is hard to jest when you feel bad. That is not strange, not out of place. For some, having fun might come off as inauthentic, so they would rather be honest with their emotions. This may be honest, but it is maybe a bit shortsighted.

The thief comes only to steal and kill and destroy. I came that they may have life and have it abundantly.
John 10:10

There is someone who is coming to steal, kill, and destroy you. He is your enemy, your foe. It is in fact the devil, and he has nothing but hate for you and wants what is worst for you. Yes, it is healthy and prudent to believe in the devil; Jesus did. Actually, he tried to take from Jesus too. He wants to steal your joy, kill your gladness, and destroy your cheer. Jesus came so that we might have a full life, and a full life is meant to be lived.

You can endure loss and still find moments of joy. People who have lost loved ones have often found joy in the smiles they miss and the glad times they had. Every day people without financial resources discover that laughter is free, and those with the least material wealth often know this best. Those under overwhelming stress can still find the comical in spite of the absolute absurdity of their situation. Fun makes life a little more bearable, so don't let the thief take anything else from you.

Challenge: Do something fun. Play a game, hang out with a friend, dance to a silly song. Play with a child. Do something fun for the fun of it!

12
WONDERFULLY MADE

D o you know how awesome you are? That is not an opinion. It's a fact! No matter how you feel, it is the truth of you. This should not be an opportunity for conceit, but a humble acceptance of reality. It is not a condition based on your parents or your own innate attractiveness; it is a gifted beauty given to you by God.

When God made you, He did not make a mistake. From your physical appearance to your personality, He did it on purpose. So many people have a problem with God's design that they see in the mirror. But, you are BEAUTIFUL! You may not like you, but God loves you so much that He made you one of one. Even twins are not completely the same.

"I praise you, for I am fearfully and wonderfully made. Wonderful are your works; my soul knows it very well."
Psalm 139:14

Too many people carry pain from others who have expressed to them that their face is not their best feature. Not to mention the taunts of "stupid" or "useless". It's not true! Don't believe the lies designed to make you feel less than God's precious creation. I know that some of the people who were supposed to give you a sense of worth were guilty of tearing you down. The time has come for you to live beyond those words.

You may need a divine reset! When you go back to the manufacturer's perspective, it helps you see yourself through His eyes. If God likes what He sees, then you have no right to tear down His treasure. You are more than you may have previously believed.

Challenge: Write down 10 positive personal attributes. Start with something you like about yourself physically, then look at internal traits. For example, "I have kind eyes" then "I am a good friend." Once you write out the list of 10, repeat it to yourself 3 times aloud today.

13

HELP IS HERE

You are not alone! You at times may feel alone, but you aren't. You may have heard the term Triune God or Trinity when it comes to God. The concept is that He is 3 in 1, Father, Son, and Holy Spirit. It may sound strange, but that is how God through His Word explains Himself. All God, all distinct, all unique, all right! If you talk to a human who is triune it's a problem, but for God to be that way is appropriate. Many people try to come up with cool ways of communicating it, maybe it's better to simply attribute this ineffability to, basically only God is God.

Jesus (The Son), gives us this relationship in the Gospel according to John. We hear Jesus speaking about the Father, who will send the Holy Spirit.

"If you love me, you will keep my commandments. And I will ask the Father, and he will give you another Helper, to be with you forever, even the Spirit of truth, whom

the world cannot receive, because it neither sees him nor knows him. You know him, for he dwells with you and will be in you." John 14:15-17

The Holy Spirit is a gift that would be sent to us from the Father, and He would HELP us. He helps by advocating for, to intercede on behalf of, in council, and comfort. He helps us live for Jesus. The Spirit would not be merely an outside observer, but would move in and lead us from the inside. So, if you are a Jesus follower, you are not alone.

So, many ignore the Holy Spirit (Ghost) because they don't understand Him, or He may feel uncomfortable with the "spooky" connotations He is given. But, He is God ready to assist. When you are in need He helps. He will bring counsel when you are unsure. In moments when you feel like you are about to break down, he will wrap His arms around you and bring loving support. God is indeed with you!

Challenge: Acknowledge His presence by praying...

Father, I thank You for the Holy Spirit. Spirit of God, I recognize that You are for me and in me. I yield to Your direction and leadership in every area of my life. I know that You are here to help me for my good and Your glory. Guide me in the way I should go, and help me when I am unsure, unstable, and unaware. In Jesus' name, amen.

14

AN END TO ANXIETY

It seems as if the whole world has become anxious. People appear to have an increased need for emotional support. Every day there is a news story about a different resource to help people manage their anxiety. The one constant thing is that no one knows why. Yes, there are personal triggers, but why does our society have this collective unease? The sad truth is, no matter what the cause, we have to individually face it to minimize its effects on our lives.

"Let your reasonableness be known to everyone. The Lord is at hand; do not be anxious about anything, but in everything by prayer and supplication with thanksgiving let your requests be made known to God. And the peace of God, which surpasses all understanding, will guard your hearts and your minds in Christ Jesus."
Philippians 4:5-7

This scripture alone has a calming effect. We don't have to be overly nervous about our circumstances because God is here. The good news is He is close, and we now have support from the God of the universe! Therefore, don't be anxious about anything ... I wish it was that simple. I am grateful that this scripture didn't stop there.

First, this text does not shame you for having anxiety. It is reminding you that you don't have to be overly stressed and distracted. But, the Bible does give us something to do.

You can pray. Tell God about the things that distress you. All of it, your worries, failures, and fears. God is big enough to handle your concerns. Do it with thanksgiving for what He has done. Yes, you want more things, but give thanks for what you have. Parents understand how amazing it is when their children don't just ask for more, but appreciate what has been given. It makes them want to give the new thing that is requested. Maybe we get that trait from our Heavenly Father.

When we learn to trust God with all the angst we feel and know that He has it covered, we have a chance to embrace the peace that goes beyond our understanding—peace that guards both our hearts and minds. Peace that stills our worries and fears. Peace, sweet peace.

Challenge: Take a moment of silence today. You know the things that tend to make your mind race. Sit still, and take a few breaths. Focus on the God who grants peace. State a biblical principle or a scripture that speaks of His goodness and love. Let that steady your mind. Relax for 2 minutes while concentrating on who He is. Do this a few times today.

15
DON'T FAINT

"For the one who sows to his own flesh will from the flesh reap corruption, but the one who sows to the Spirit will from the Spirit reap eternal life. And let us not grow weary of doing good, for in due season we will reap, if we do not give up." Galatians 6:8-9

Our scripture today starts right where most people have the hardest time following God: we all battle with this thing called the flesh. More than a few have started down the road of darkness by simply yielding to one fleshly desire. The idea of the flesh is that our own desires are the things that betray us in an effort to abandon God's will. It's sneaky; it uses us to destroy us. The more we give in to that pull, we pull away from God's best for us.

The good news is that the opposite is true as well. The more we yield to the Spirit, the more we avoid the desires that would wreck our lives. The solution is to keep following God and to resist evil, even if doing evil feels right. It is shocking how evil, as defined by the Bible, feels right and comfortable. That is what the flesh is all about. Know that you are not the only one who has been tempted to give in to your sinful earthly desires. This is in part what it means to be human. God has a better way, and better things for you than your flesh would lead you to believe.

Don't be discouraged if you have been struggling with the same issues for a while. Don't give up! If you have given your life to Jesus, you win if you don't give in. It is easy to want to throw in the towel because you don't see the progress you would like to see. You don't win because you are good at mitigating your sin. Victory is not made possible through your ability. You win because Jesus' sacrifice ensures your success, eternally. HALLELUJAH!

What is expected from you is that you not give up! You can stumble every day of your life, but refuse to quit. Keep fighting forward. You will get a reward that you would never be able to earn, if you just keep trying and trusting.

Challenge: Look in a mirror and say to yourself, "Don't you give up!" Repeat this action 5 times today.

16

PAYMENT IN FULL

D ebt is difficult. To owe someone else feels as if your life is one hold while you are figuring out how to make the repayment. Debt is often unavoidable, for example, when people need to purchase a house or pay for college tuition. In those instances, when the balance is paid, most people experience a sense of relief and satisfaction and freedom.

Our relationship with God has a similar tone. Not because God is not good, but because our sin is that bad.

"But now the righteousness of God has been manifested apart from the law, although the Law and the Prophets bear witness to it— the righteousness of God through faith in Jesus Christ for all who believe. For there is no distinction: for all have sinned and fall short of the glory of God, and are justified by his grace as a gift, through the redemption that is in Christ Jesus, whom God put forward as a propitiation by his blood, to be

received by faith. This was to show God's righteousness,
because in his divine forbearance he had passed over
former sins." Romans 3:21-25

God's perfect justice is revealed to us in Jesus. We were born with an enduring debt called sin. This legacy existed within all men in Adam and Eve's original failure, but God's goodness stepped in to end it. That is comforting in so many ways. Everyone falls short of the glory of God; you aren't the only one. We have a shared brokenness.

That is why His grace, not ours, made our payment possible. His kindness and favor that we could not afford stepped in on our behalf.

Jesus' was our propitiation—that is, payment in full! God's justice was that Jesus' blood shed so that ours would not. He paid the balance for our faults so that we could live in freedom. That was for our best, and it was all God's idea. No longer do we have to live with the crushing weight of what we owe. We don't get a choice in whether this is true: when Jesus yelled, "IT IS FINISHED," it truly was.

Now we get to live without impending doom hovering over us. That is how good God is. He paid our debt, and now we get to live in His freedom. And to God, that is justice. All we need to do is accept this extravagant gift offered by the Extravagant One!

Challenge: Do something outside today to remind you of your freedom in Christ. Whether it means taking a walk, paying attention to all the beautiful colors. Go for a bike ride. If the weather is inclement or if you are physically incapable of going out, then sit at a window, look out in awe at God's creation!

17

BE STILL

"**D**o more" seems to be the motto of far too many nowadays. We believe that the best way to move forward is by hard work. There is no substitute for hard work. The back side of that concept is just as powerful. That is, with all your hard work you should trust that God can take care of everything that is too big for you. There are some issues that are perfectly God sized. To strike a healthy balance between these two ideas is more of an art than a science.

"Be still, and know that I am God. I will be exalted among the nations, I will be exalted in the earth!"
Psalm 46:10

To be still takes the same amount of discipline that the failure of busyness does. Moments of quietness in the presence of God is a good thing. To reflect and trust is a spiritual practice that helps believers slow down enough to remember that God will be lifted, whether we participate or not. God's will, will come to pass in your life. A good work ethic is Biblical, but also is being still and knowing who your God is and what He can do. We need to be reminded that God wants our involvement and gives us the chance to help in this work. But, it will happen either way. Far too many pastors fail at accomplishing stillness.

Simply stated, sometimes you are supposed to labor with great intensity. Then to recover from that effort you must trust God to actually bring success as you stop and still your heart and mind to concentrate on Him. This is how the scriptures encourage Jesus followers to meditate. Be careful, because we live in a culture that has many varied perspectives on the notion of meditation. This is biblical meditation, and it is different than what this world offers. Regardless of how they see practice, we for our spiritual and mental health must find a good rhythm of stillness and work.

Challenge: Take 3, two-minute moments to still your heart and mind today. Find a scriptural truth to focus on and think about that for the two-minute duration. Sit in silence, take a few deep breaths, meditate on the Biblical truth and allow your heart to focus on God.

18
PROTECT YOUR HEART

*"Keep your heart with all vigilance,
for from it flow the springs of life". Proverb 4:23*

The heart s an exhaustible resource. The emotional heart is this proverbial inner place of feelings and passions. We treat it as if it is the anatomical heart, but it's not. I wonder if that's because nothing gets the pump in our chest beating like something that inspires our proverbial heart. The Bible talks about this emotional heart a lot. We need a new one to follow Jesus. We shouldn't harden it, and it is so important that we must guard it.

Protecting one's own heart is more challenging than we like to think. There are so many fleeting desires at war for your affections. Lust, greed, and anger, to name a few, are constantly assaulting us. Keep people who don't have your best interest at heart at a distance. Guard your heart!

Proverb 4:23 does not say that you must protect yourself from outside forces alone. People often fail to see the less obvious danger facing the heart. That danger comes from the heart itself. There are things that you must keep from you for your ultimate good. This is why it is essential to have at least one other person in your life to whom you can be accountable. It is healthy to have someone that we give permission to challenge and remind us of who we are and the commitments we have made to God. Sometimes we need to protect ourselves from ourselves.

Keeping watch over your heart can be very difficult. It is all about creating restrictions on yourself to ensure your emotional and mental health. You have to admit how flawed you are and admit that you have a propensity to mess things up. It's all about placing guards on yourself so that you don't lead yourself astray. Our hearts are naturally wicked. The process of creating barriers for our own protection is a good thing. This is not someone else controlling you; this is you shielding yourself from the unhealthy influences that compete for your attention. To become a mature Jesus follower, you must develop the ability to do this. Please, guard your heart!

Challenge: Write down the top 5 issues that challenge your commitment to God. For each one, write down at least 2 things that will keep you safe from engaging in practices that endanger your soul. For example, if you keep getting in bad romantic relationships, you may need to have someone you trust check the person out before you get serious. If you have issues with alcohol, you may need to decide to abstain from it altogether. This will help you develop a healthy rhythm of creating guards for your heart.

19

SHEEP, NEED A GOOD SHEPHERD

I f you have been around church or the Christian community, you would have most likely heard the analogy of believers to sheep. When you live in an urban or suburban area, this may go over your head. Understanding how sheep interact with one another and with their shepherd is important for this concept to make sense.

For one thing, sheep have very little skill or ability to protect themselves. They are largely vulnerable to being ravaged by predators. They are mostly communal creatures. Their safety is in their numbers. This is common in animals with herd animals with little defensive skills. Sheer numbers confuse and overwhelm attacking raiders.

As believers, we are supposed to flock together as well. As sheep, we don't always have the protection we need from things that desire to devour us. There are forces that want to scatter us because we are easier to pick off one by one. Jesus leaned into this sheep and shepherd illustration. He says that He is our shepherd, and not an average one.

I am the good shepherd. The good shepherd lays down his life for the sheep. He who is a hired hand and not a shepherd, who does not own the sheep, sees the wolf coming and leaves the sheep and flees, and the wolf snatches them and scatters them. He flees because he is a hired hand and cares nothing for the sheep. I am the good shepherd. I know my own and my own know me, just as the Father knows me and I know the Father; and I lay down my life for the sheep. John 10:11-15

When we stand together with our good shepherd, we are protected by the very life of that good one! It is for our good that we are supposed to stand in community with other believers. We are in a time when congregating in a spiritual community is a low priority. It should be very important to us because it is for our safety. This kind of gathering is of course called the church. We come up with inventive ways to make excuses for why we don't need to meet regularly in a church setting. Some people have quipped, "I don't go to church; I am the church!" This is not true. One person cannot be the church, because the word itself is plural. It is an assembly of people who meet for the sake of Jesus, and He promises to protect them with His very life. We are the sheep under a good shepherd.

Challenge: Reach out to someone within your local church body(community) for the purpose of encouragement. If you are not in a healthy church, find one. Do some research today on good churches in your area. One easy way to do this is to look to someone you know that is living well for Jesus. They are probably connected to a healthy local community. Let's be good sheep for our good shepherd, Jesus.

20
SHEPHERD-LESS

O ne of the most memorized chapters in the entire Bible is Psalm 23. This chapter is required reading at funerals within the church and in most funeral homes. It has been widely accepted as a source of comfort for the mourning and troubled soul. It is good to know that God is with you when you feel scared or alone. If we are going to be encouraged, we should listen to what has done that for God's people for thousands of years.

"The Lord is my shepherd; I shall not want. He makes me lie down in green pastures. He leads me beside still waters. He restores my soul. He leads me in paths of righteousness for his name's sake. Even though I walk through the valley of the shadow of death, I will fear no evil, for you are with me; your rod and your staff, they comfort me. You prepare a table before me in the presence of my enemies; you anoint my head with oil; my cup overflows. Surely goodness and mercy shall follow

*me all the days of my life, and I shall dwell in the house
of the Lord forever." Psalm 23*

Widely attributed to King David, this poem speaks to the fear and desperation we all come to at some point in our lives. Whether we face loss, anxiety, or lack of clarity and direction, the psalm is powerful. It keeps reminding us that we have a good shepherd who guides us even when we feel hopeless.

The idea of a God being a Shepherd is a very old one. Jacob, one of the patriarchs of the Judeo-Christian foundation beliefs, said, "God has been my Shepherd all my life." This point is lost to a modern world. A shepherd guided his sheep to good places to eat. He would also protect his flock from wandering off, mend wounds, and even fight off wolves, bears, mountain lions, and wild dogs. A herdsman's livelihood and worth were tied to the safety and success of the sheep. This relationship was so close that the sheep would know their shepherd's voice over others, and they could even distinguish the smell of their keeper. All these traits give you insights into the close-knit relationship between the sheep and their shepherd.

This connection is good news for us, the precious ones who desperately need guidance and protection. For we are valuable to the one who risks His life for us. We are God's sheep! To not have this link with a loving defender leaves us vulnerable, lost, and harassed. This should break our hearts for those who don't know

Him. To get a glimpse of their current state, read this reversed telling of the psalm to gain understanding of a shepherd-less person.

"The Lord is [not] my shepherd; I shall [have nothing but] want.
[I never] lie down in green pastures.
[I am never] beside still waters.
[My soul is never restored].
[I wander in paths of darkness for no reason]
[When I] walk through the valley of the shadow of death, [I fear evil],
For [no one is] with me; [no rod or staff, comfort me.]
[No one prepares] a table before me, [I am] in the presence of my enemies;
[No one anoints] my head with oil;
my cup [is empty].
Surely [evil and vengeance] shall follow me all the days of my life,
and I shall dwell [alone] forever."
It is a gift to know and be known by our Great Shepherd.

Challenge: Read Psalm 23. Read it 3 times today and thank God for being your shepherd.

57

21
PERFECTION

*"Count it all joy, my brothers, when you meet trials of
various kinds, for you know that the testing of your
faith produces steadfastness. ⁴ And let steadfastness have
its full effect, that you may be perfect and complete,
lacking in nothing." James 1:2-4*

Sometimes it feels like the Bible asks us to do too
much. Are we really supposed to experience joy
in the midst of challenges? This scripture compounds
things as it points to the truth that we may have to
face multiple tests at the same time. This sounds impossible—and it is, if you are hyper-focused on a current
hardship. The good news is that *James 1:2-4* gives us
God's perspective which benefits us greatly.

These trials we must face produce more than just pain.
They develop our faith! That is pretty amazing. But, it
does not stop there. That faith then creates patience
(steadfastness). Patience gives us the ability to remain

constant no matter what comes our way. This should not be overlooked nor discounted. Our endurance in discomfort allows us to enjoy life when our circumstances would normally cause us to quit. It's like a person who starts doing strength training. It takes a while to develop the muscles needed to bear heavy loads. The pain experienced in the process has a point, to help someone grow stronger. The battles that must be endured now, develop in us the ability to overcome future struggles. All of the things we encounter are working to make us perfect!

Perfection is a dirty word, I know. But, here it doesn't mean what you may think it means. Perfect in this context means *mature*. It basically means that God wants His people to grow up. Too many believers are content throwing tantrums and complaining because their life is not what they wished it were. We must grow up spiritually! In our culture, perfection is the notion of flawlessness. That is not the truth here. That is what we will be once we see Jesus face to face. Until then, let us continue to grow in our faith, becoming mature enough to withstand anything that might come our way.

Challenge: Take a moment to think about the areas in which you need to grow spiritually. Write them down and make them a prayer focus today. Whether it is a bad attitude, an unhealthy habit, or a lack of desire to engage in spiritual discipline, ask God to give you the stamina necessary to mature in your faith.

22

IMAGO DEI

You are special. You were made for a reason. You bear the very image of God. When God made you, He did not make a mistake. He knows exactly what you look like. He was intentional about your personality. There is the likelihood that the very things you hate about yourself, God loves.

When fighting to remain hopeful, it is important that we embrace the *imago dei*, the image of God.

"So God created man in his own image, in the image of God he created him; male and female he created them."
Genesis 1:27

This means that every person carries the fingerprint of God in them. He has endowed us with Himself. You don't have to be a Jesus follower for this to be true. People who look differently, think differently, live differently than you all have this in common. That person that you don't like—it is true of them too. Consider the traits you deem abhorrent, whether someone is bucked toothed, pockmarked, too short, too tall, too talkative, too quiet, too much for you. They are just enough for God.

Human beings can create inventive ways of robbing others of this dignity. The Holocaust happened because a population was convinced that Jewish people were subhuman. The Rwandan genocide was powered by the images of people as roaches. Not to mention slavery of all types, where one person literally owns another, benefiting from their labor. Sex trafficking is a form of slavery, too. Rape and murder take from fellow image bearers: one robbing from both body and soul, and the other taking the very life. None of these crimes are comprehensible when you see Almighty God reflected back at you in the face of others.

We all carry the signature of the Creator God. It elevates us and should serve to empower us. It enables us to both love ourselves and others. When you look in the mirror, you should love what you see, because you are God's handiwork. When you find it hard to recognize beauty in another, remember they bear His image as well. This is one of the most basic failures of believers: we can quickly fail to see God in individuals with whom we disagree. That is not their fault; it's ours. When we don't appreciate the reality of His image within each person, including ourselves, we fail to embrace the truth of who we are.

Challenge: First, tell yourself over and over, "I am made in God's image, and He did not make a mistake with me." Second, when interacting with someone you have a hard time seeing His beauty in, declare to them, "You are made in the image of God. He did not make a mistake with you."

23

THE WRESTLE

L ife can be hard sometimes. Someone once said, "Either you are going through a storm, you just came out of one, or you're about to go through one." That might not be completely true, but it sure feels that way. The people who usually have an easier time with life's ups and downs are those who have had a history filled with a tougher journey. No one can control the family they grew up in. The quality of that foundation will often create expectations that shape how we see and interact with the world.

Some people feel like they have to fight for everything. Others expect everything to be given to them on a silver platter. We learn these lessons early, and they can have a major impact on our outlook. How we grow beyond these early lessons can determine the kind of people we will become.

One of the major patriarchs of the faith is a good example of this kind of conditioning. When it comes to the patriarchs, God calls Himself the God of Abraham, Isaac, and Jacob. All of these men were completely flawed, but God used them anyway. The last one, Jacob, seemed to be the most wayward. His name means deceiver. He was a master manipulator. He cheated his older twin brother out of his inheritance. He even with the help of his mother (because he was her favorite), swindled his brother's blessing out of his father. Jacob was not always a good guy. He depended on his ability to connive and outsmart others to thrive. God would ultimately teach him a lesson from which Jacob would never recover.

"And Jacob was left alone. And a man wrestled with him until the breaking of the day. When the man saw that he did not prevail against Jacob, he touched his hip socket, and Jacob's hip was put out of joint as he wrestled with him. Then he said, "Let me go, for the day has broken." But Jacob said, "I will not let you go unless you bless me." And he said to him, "What is your name?" And he said, "Jacob." Then he said, "Your name shall no longer be called Jacob, but Israel, for you have striven with God and with men, and have prevailed."
Genesis 32:24-28

After this encounter with a messenger from God, Jacob would no longer be able to depend on his own ability to make things happen. He ran into someone he could not manipulate. He would have a limp that would be a constant reminder that he needed to live differently. He also received a name change for this same reason. No longer would he be Jacob the deceiver; he would be Israel, which means God strives. It was no longer up to him to figure his life out. God would fight for him and make things happen. He would have to be dependent. Just as he had to depend on a staff to walk, he needed God to live.

Every believer must "wrestle" with God in at least one area. For most people, this contest of wills covers multiple areas, and people must fight often for each one. This is a part of our devotion that must be given its proper attention. We are all a little like Jacob. But God, instead of destroying us—as He could have done with Jacob—increases our dependence on Him. Even if it means that He has to wrestle with us, it's for our own good.

Challenge: Do you have part of your life that is solely dependent on you? In which areas are you wrestling with God because of your unhealthy ways of functioning? It could be connected to a sin that has dominated your life or a part of your thinking that you haven't surrendered to God. Write down every area you have yet to yield to God. Confess those faults to God in prayer and ask for His forgiveness.

24

MESSING UP

W ho wants to be wrong, broken, messed up inside? No one. The truth is that we are all broken in some way or another. There is no escaping it. We have human flaws. It's a waste of time to deny the sad reality of our human condition. It is so much easier to simply embrace it as a part of life and to move forward.

It's frustrating to be around a person who refuses to be wrong. You know the kind of people who have excuses for everything. If they are late, it's because someone didn't tell them that there would be traffic. If they break something, somebody should have mentioned that it was slippery. If they have a spot on their clothes, it is the restaurant's fault for not giving them adequate warning about that particular meal. Some individuals refuse to be wrong about anything.

This is not the approach of a believer. Jesus followers are supposed to be wired differently. We are those who confess our faults and take responsibility for our mistakes. This is not a new concept; it is all throughout the Bible. David was both king and flawed. Many of the rival kings of his day would be deified and considered infallible. David was a murderer and an adulterer. When he finally had to face his sin, this was his prayer.

"Create in me a clean heart, O God, and renew a right spirit within me. Cast me not away from your presence, and take not your Holy Spirit from me. Restore to me the joy of your salvation, and uphold me with a willing spirit. Then I will teach transgressors your ways, and sinners will return to you. Deliver me from bloodguiltiness, O God, O God of my salvation, and my tongue will sing aloud of your righteousness. O Lord, open my lips, and my mouth will declare your praise."
Psalm 51:10-15

David not only confessed his guilt for his sin. He wrote it down for us to read. It would forever be preserved that even someone as great at David messed up royally. He is literally in this psalm teaching readers about his mistakes, and while David's words are poetic, they still represent his failure to adhere to God's way. He was more concerned about being in a healthy relationship with God than he was worried about how history would perceive him. This is an example to follow!

Yes, you will make mistakes. Yes, you are flawed and sinful. Yes, you will be wrong at times. Yes, God will forgive you and help you to try to do better next time! Don't try to avoid your brokenness. Use it to bring you closer to a God who knows it already and is waiting for you to confess it.

Challenge: Confess a personal struggle to God and a good, reliable, and trustworthy friend or loved one. Don't make any excuses for your bad behavior. Own it and give it to God. Ask the other person to pray for you and with you as you endeavor to be better.

25

BETRAYAL

People can be the worst. It is frustrating how much God created us to rely on others. As much as we love the people in our lives, they can let us down. Any abused child can tell you that. The ones we rely on the most can hurt us the deepest. They lie, cheat, steal, and betray. If we are honest, we have those tendencies too. But when we are on the receiving end of other people's failures, it is painful.

Joseph knew what it was like to be betrayed by those you love. He was the favorite son of a large family filled with boys. His dad gave him a coat of many colors that was probably better than anything he gave his other sons. Joseph was also a bit of a tattletale and a braggart. But, what little brother isn't? He would have elaborate dreams about being so great that his entire family would bow before him. Okay, that was bad!

Joseph's father sent him to find his brothers and report on them. When Joseph went to spy on his brothers, they saw him coming and plotted to kill him. Instead, they sold him into slavery. There are bratty little siblings and we pinch, kick (when no one is looking), and grow tired of them. To sell your own brother into slavery is another thing altogether.

Joseph would be a slave in a rich man's house. He was in fact exceptional and thrived under unbelievable circumstances. Eventually, his master's wife decided that he was awfully handsome and she wanted to sleep with him. Joseph refused her and ran away, and she lied about what happened, saying he tried to rape her. Joseph was thrown in jail. But through an amazing series of events, he later became the second most powerful man in the world.

Joseph would spend 18 years enslaved and imprisoned all because he was betrayed by his brothers. Joseph had his issues, yes, but the brothers are without question simply horrible. After 22 years, we see Joseph's dream come to pass. His brothers would ultimately bow before him. After he rescued his entire family, his dad died. His brothers thought he was about to repay them for all of the suffering they caused him, and his response was powerful.

"Say to Joseph, 'Please forgive the transgression of your brothers and their sin, because they did evil to you.'" And now, please forgive the transgression of the

servants of the God of your father.' Joseph wept when
they spoke to him. His brothers also came and fell
down before him and said, 'Behold, we are your ser-
vants.' But Joseph said to them, 'Do not fear, for am I
in the place of God? As for you, you meant evil against
me, but God meant it for good, to bring it about that
many people should be kept alive, as they are today.
So do not fear; I will provide for you and your little
ones.' Thus he comforted them and spoke kindly to them.
Genesis 50:17-21

After his brothers' betrayal, Joseph forgave them. After all those years, he saw God's purpose even through pain. His brothers devised evil, but God's plan prevailed. God didn't waste Joseph's pain. Even when you are betrayed and treated poorly by those who are supposed to love you, God has a plan for you, too. Your painful experiences don't have to define you any longer. You must be like Joseph, because life is too short to allow what happens to you to define you. Your life is too important to waste on that pain anymore.

Challenge: Set a chair across from you, and imagine a person or people sitting across from you who have done you wrong. Tell them how they have hurt you, and tell them that you refuse to carry the anguish they have caused you. This is a healthy way to process your pain.

26
GOD SEES

G od sees you and He cares. When enduring dark seasons, our souls want to know that God is not distant. We don't always even need to get the answer we want. Just to know that Someone mighty, infinite, and compassionate is present in hard times is often enough. The warm feelings we have come to recognize as God's presence, if we are honest, are unreliable. Not that He is unreliable, but the goosebumps we associate with Him are.

What do we do, then, when we don't have the emotional connection we once did? The answer is to believe what the Bible says. It is the Word of God, and He speaks clearly through it. So, what does it say? Jesus reminded us of the fact that we are not alone, even when we feel alone.

"Are not two sparrows sold for a penny? And not one of them will fall to the ground apart from your Father. But even the hairs of your head are all numbered. Fear

not, therefore; you are of more value than many spar-
rows. Matthew 10:29-31

Jesus here reminds us that we are seen by our Heavenly Father. He is a good Father, so He is vigilant and filled with love. He keeps His eyes on His own. So even if you feel like He doesn't see you, Jesus said He does, so that is that. God is so intimately connected to what is going on with you that He has the hairs on your head numbered. For some that is more challenging than others, but the Father has them counted.

We don't have to be afraid! We don't have to worry about God's proximity or His perspective. He is always near and always interested. Why? Jesus says it's because we are valuable to God. You matter to Him. We all do. We are His children, and He sees us. He cares and He is for us. He is for you.

If what you are experiencing on the inside does not agree with Jesus, then what you are sensing is lying to you. The Word of God is true! Jesus did not and does not deceive us. If our Father in heaven were not interested in us, then Jesus would have told us so.

Challenge: Leave yourself note on either your bathroom or bedroom mirror in soap, shaving cream, lipstick, etc. That note should say, "God sees me, and I am valuable to Him." The point is to repeatedly remind yourself of this Biblical principle.

27
FRIENDS

We were not meant to live isolated from others. Yes, the hardest part of dealing with people is, in fact, the people. The truth is, we are not so great either. We are flawed, and just as we have to endure the faults of others, they must do the same for us. That does not change the fact that we need friends.

"Two are better than one, because they have a good reward for their toil. For if they fall, one will lift up his fellow. But woe to him who is alone when he falls and has not another to lift him up! Again, if two lie together, they keep warm, but how can one keep warm alone? And though a man might prevail against one who is alone, two will withstand him—a threefold cord is not quickly broken." Ecclesiastes 4:9-12

To be able to depend on another human being is a gift. To have someone to lighten our proverbial load is a good thing. Who has your back, and who's back do you have? We all need someone. The person who refuses to have friends is a person who chooses to sabotage themselves.

You don't have to have a lot of friends, but you need at least one. Life is hard enough without adding to it by choosing to live absent of others. Not every personality is complementary to yours. Not everyone can or should be trusted with your heart. But, it is critical for your natural and spiritual development to have someone. For some it's a spouse; others have siblings or parents. But we all have this need, and denying that only hurts us.

It can be hard developing new relationships. If you move into a new community or are estranged from those you used to engage with, it is difficult to start anew. But it must be done. At least one other person should be given permission to hold your heart and you theirs.

Challenge: If you have a good friend, spouse, parent, sibling, etc. with whom you can share your deepest thoughts, reach out to them today. Let them know that you appreciate and care for them. If you are struggling to invite others into your confidence, identify 2 people who have the potential of being a close friend and start a simple dialog with them about interest. You make friends by being friendly.

28

STRONG AND COURAGEOUS

"This Book of the Law shall not depart from your mouth,
but you shall meditate on it day and night, so that you
may be careful to do according to all that is written in it.
For then you will make your way prosperous, and then
you will have good success. Have I not commanded you?
Be strong and courageous. Do not be frightened, and
do not be dismayed, for the Lord your God is with you
wherever you go." Joshua 1:8-10

This encouragement came straight from God for a new leader who was being prepared to lead God's people. He was told what was necessary, which was to remain faithful to Scripture. Without the written word of God, a person is just a loud fanatic making it up as they go. This is God telling him that His Word was critical to Joshua's and the people's success. This is true of us as well.

Be both strong and courageous. This is obviously necessary, because Joshua was feeling weak and scared. It makes sense considering they were about to entire a new territory that they had to fight for. As Moses' protégé he had seen how stubborn and rebellious this large group he was commissioned to lead was. God was asking him to do a nearly impossible task. He watched Moses, the greatest leader he had ever seen, grow increasingly frustrated with them. He was also one of two people from his whole generation who would be seeing this new land that God had promised, so he was leading young people who had yet to prove their strength and faithfulness. Of course, Joshua was feeling nervous.

In spite of how Joshua felt, he still had to move forward with confidence. Then we start to understand why he could take on this monumental task. God was with him and would lead him forward. As long as Joshua was in alignment with God's direction he would see His favor.

This story should give you courage when you are note sure you can move forward. There will undoubtedly be times when you feel so overwhelmed and unsure if you can continue. We have tasks that require more than we think we can handle. We can rest assured that when we adhere to Scripture and follow God's leading, we can be both strong and courageous.

Challenge: Write down all the tasks that you are facing that seem too big for you to handle. For each one, write the encouragement from Joshua chapter 1 below it: *Be strong and courageous. Do not be frightened, and do not be dismayed, for the Lord your God is with you wherever you go.*

29

HEALTHY LAMENT

"Now when Mary came to where Jesus was and saw him, she fell at his feet, saying to him, "Lord, if you had been here, my brother would not have died." When Jesus saw her weeping, and the Jews who had come with her also weeping, he was deeply moved in his spirit and greatly troubled. And he said, "Where have you laid him?" They said to him, "Lord, come and see." Jesus wept. So the Jews said, "See how he loved him!" John 11:32-26

*J*esus wept. Officially it is the shortest single verse in the whole Bible. It may be small, but it is saturated with significance and insight. By embracing the context, we may be able to understand why this is so important. The circumstances around this verse are truly fascinating.

At this point, Jesus' friend Lazarus had died days ago, and Jesus had finally arrived at the scene. He was asked to rush to the side of his friend, as all knew His reputation as a healer. Therefore, Jesus stayed longer, by doing this He made sure that Lazarus not only died, but had started to decay. That may not seem like the correct response from a loving friend, not to mention God in human flesh. But He had a plan, just not the plan they expected.

By the time Jesus arrives, everyone is mourning, and almost are blaming him for His obvious lack of urgency. You can hear it in Mary's tone that they believed with all of their hearts that Jesus could have healed Lazarus no matter the sickness. His response is so jarring: he cries. Not in a stern, masculine, one solitary teardrop down the cheek way, but deep mourning that proved to the onlookers that He loved His friend.

If you have not read this story, Jesus would raise Lazarus from the dead, in spectacular form too. He waited to do it and knew he would. So why did He weep? Jesus showed us how to mourn! He demonstrated how to lament the loss of a loved one, that it was okay to grieve in grievous situations. He grieved even though He knew the outcome. Jesus showed compassion by identifying with the loss of others. He didn't try to minimize something that hurt. He embraced it!

To lament and mourn is healthy and good. It gives significance to the life lost, the opportunity missed, and the change to be expected. To feel deeply is to be human. There is a whole book of the Bible focused on the beauty and necessity of mourning; it's called

Lamentations. David suffered grief and loss also. Many of the Psalms focus their attention on this vital human process. Jeremiah mourned the sin and consequences of the people of God rebelling against God so much that some scholars considered Him depressed. Have you given yourself permission to lament? If not, there are a lot of people in the Scriptures who are offering you that opportunity. Time does not heal wounds; process does.

Challenge: Cry! Be sad! Take some time to be by yourself and feel bad about the things that are worthy of this healthy emotional response. It's not weakness, because Jesus was not weak! Allow your tears or your sadness to address these critical feelings and if possible, wash it away.

30
TRUST IS FAITH

One of the hardest things to do for so many is to trust another person. This is often for many reasons. For some it connects to a trauma that has sadly been experienced. Another may struggle with trust put in themselves which is an overestimation of one's own abilities. The problem is that we project on God the issues that create our lack of trust. No matter the source, we have to learn to trust others, and it starts with trusting God.

"Trust in the Lord with all your heart, and do not lean on your own understanding. In all your ways acknowledge him, and he will make straight your paths."
Proverb 3:5-6

Trusting God with your whole heart is tough. What if He lets me down? What if He doesn't come through for me the way I anticipate or the way I was told He would? To start, you have to reset your expectations.

God is good, and that is a perfect place to begin. To know that He is good starts the process, because we can allow our circumstances to make us quietly start believing that He is not.

Too often we blame God for the failures of others, and He is guilty in our minds because of what others have done. "If He is good, He would not have allowed "that" to happen to me." This is a very real obstacle to many people's faith. This is why the Bible is so important. When we listen to secondhand knowledge about God without getting to know Him through His Word, then we can believe false narratives that are given to us. For instance, many Biblical figures who have experienced seemingly unbearable hardship have written about God's goodness. So, why would we believe that these two ideas can't exist at the same time? God can be immeasurably good and life be ridiculously difficult simultaneously. The more you read Scripture, the more these false perspectives start to fall away.

We can have faith in God because He is faithful. Without faith we can't even get into a pleasing relationship with God. Wait, weren't we talking about trust? Yes, you see, faith and trust are the same thing. The Old Testament used the word trust in the same way that the New Testament uses the word faith. Both mean that God can be depended upon, relied on, or stood upon without breaking. When we lean on our own understanding we trust ourselves, but the Bible tells us to lean on God and He will work things out?

You may not fully trust God, but He is inviting you to do so. He wants to make sure that your life fulfills its intended destiny, even if you don't know what it is yet. He knows and He has the path laid out for you. It may include some unpleasantness, but He will lead you to where you ultimately are supposed to be. What about the pain that makes you nervous to trust anyone? He has a way of using that pain for your greater purpose. He often heals us as He walks with us the path, He has laid for us.

Challenge: Read the story of Joseph in Genesis 37-45. This is a story of someone who endured hardship but discovered God's providence despite the pain.

31

POST VICTORY
POUTING

Have you noticed how often some people will have a great victory and immediately fall into sadness? Many pastors face the Monday blues after a phenomenal Sunday worship experience. That is one reason why we need to pray for pastors. They have an emotionally demanding job. But, this dynamic is not that strange when you look at biblical history. Elijah experienced a similar moment. God had recently brought victory through him in a faceoff of prophets. Elijah versus the prophets of Baal was a lopsided battle. 450 to 1, but the 1, Elijah had God on his side. That makes him the majority. Elijah wins in spectacular fashion and he was probably assuming that this was the moment evil was going to be dealt with once and for all. Days later he was hiding, afraid of the wicked queen's wrath.

*"Ahab told Jezebel all that Elijah had done, and how he
had killed all the prophets with the sword. Then Jezebel
sent a messenger to Elijah, saying, 'So may the gods
do to me and more also, if I do not make your life as
the life of one of them by this time tomorrow.' Then he
was afraid, and he arose and ran for his life and came
to Beersheba, which belongs to Judah, and left his servant there. But he himself went a day's journey into the
wilderness and came and sat down under a broom tree.
And he asked that he might die, saying, 'It is enough;
now, O Lord, take away my life, for I am no better than
my fathers.' And he lay down and slept under a broom
tree. And behold, an angel touched him and said to
him, 'Arise and eat.'" 1 Kings 19:1-5*

How Elijah found himself at such a low state after a victory is a study in human nature. He was questioning his
very life after being used by God to do the impossible.
Yet, when the results didn't match his expectation, he
was emotionally distraught. How did I get here? How
did my life come to this? Why would you let me come
to such a low place, God? These are all real feelings and
questions we must wrestle with from time to time, but
if we open up our hearts and minds to our God, He
will hold us even then.

Elijah went from being this powerful prophetic force
to a whimpering coward. He went from standing alone
for God against seemingly insurmountable odds to
hiding in a wilderness. We can experience the same
thing after what seems like victories. It should give us

courage that if someone so great can quickly become this weak then we might want to give ourselves a little grace for being the same way.

Notice the response from God's messenger. A touch. Not a slap, or an abrupt shout. A gentle touch. God would eventually get Elijah's attention in a more remarkable way, but it started with a touch. God's representative was so close that He could touch him. Elijah probably felt so far from God, but He was close enough for a touch. Then he was nourished and strengthened by what God prepared just for him. That is not how we see God. We see Him as a mean being, waiting to get us for our moments of fear, doubt, and worry. What if you saw God as a patient Heavenly Father who loves you even at your worst? A God who is close and has enough grace for all of your weaknesses, because that is exactly who He is.

Challenge: Read 1 Kings 18 and 19.

32
ENDURING HARDSHIP

The Apostle Paul wrote most of the New Testament. He went from being a loud opposition and a persecutor of the early church to its most known voice. He was a Pharisee, which means that he was amongst those who were considered the most spiritual. But, when he came face to face with Jesus after the resurrection everything changed. He was truly transformed and would embark on spreading the news of Jesus as far as possible.

What you may not know is that Paul also struggled with a physical ailment. No one is exactly sure what it was, but the one whom God would use to heal others would have to live with his infirmity.

"Three times I pleaded with the Lord about this, that it should leave me. But he said to me, 'My grace is sufficient for you, for my power is made perfect in weakness.' Therefore I will boast all the more gladly of

my weaknesses, so that the power of Christ may rest upon me. For the sake of Christ, then, I am content with weaknesses, insults, hardships, persecutions, and calamities. For when I am weak, then I am strong." 2 Corinthians 12:8-10

Here we learn that God knows what is best. Just because we pray for something does not mean that we get what we want. Paul didn't get what he wanted; he got something better. He received a reason that the suffering was worth it. God would use his pain for the glory of God. This is a major mark of spiritual maturity. How you are able to endure hardship reveals your development in Christ. Paul made his physical struggle a point of praise. He cared more about God's plan than his own comfort. In this way he was a powerful example for us.

How often do you complain at the slightest hint of discomfort? What would other people think about your God by how you handle your battles? Do you complain first and pray later? The fact that Paul prayed about what he was enduring should be a model to many of us. What if God says, no, or the gentler, you have grace and that is enough? How do you respond to hardship? Instead of making excuses for what we wished would change, what if we praised God in the midst of it? How different would our lives be if we followed Paul's example?

Paul didn't even stop at his infirmity. He decided to be content in all manners of tough times. He stood firm in his faith when insulted, when beaten and imprisoned, and when life was just hard. He would use all of his difficulties to increase his devotion to Jesus. His weakness would serve to help him rely on God even more.

Challenge: Refuse to complain today. Don't say anything negative about yourself or your less than desirable circumstances. If tempted, turn the conversation toward the love of God in the light of Jesus Christ.

33

SERVING OTHERS

S erving others is a gift and a prerequisite for us to achieve spiritual maturity. It is grace and mercy in action. If you see a believer who refuses to serve others, it's more likely you've seen someone who may not be a believer at all. Yes, it is that serious! This does not mean that we will always want to serve others, but that service is an expected response. Jesus served, so we serve.

The Bible has many things that we are supposed to do for one another. Love one another, pray for one another, give to one another, and serve one another are all on the list. Jesus even stresses the idea to His disciples many times. Their greatness would be determined by how they served others. Peter, one of Jesus' best friends and closest followers, emphasized this concept.

"Show hospitality to one another without grumbling. As each has received a gift, use it to serve one another, as good stewards of God's varied grace: whoever speaks, as

one who speaks oracles of God; whoever serves, as one who serves by the strength that God supplies—in order that in everything God may be glorified through Jesus Christ. To him belong glory and dominion forever and ever. Amen." 1 Peter 4:9-11

Peter added that service should be without grumbling. Does that disqualify you? This is important because we can do nice things for others while complaining the entire time. How do you feel when someone does something kind and moans while they do it? It robs the experience, doesn't it? As God has empowered us with spiritual gifts, we are to use those gifts in service to others.

Service is an issue of stewardship, meaning that God gives you the responsibility over the gifts He has given you. You then in turn use those same abilities to help someone else. To not faithfully use the resources with which you have been entrusted is theft!

If God has given you strength, use it to help others. If you can cut grass, cook food, sit at a bedside, take out the garbage, provide necessary transportation, give wholesome companionship, etc. do it! You don't have to think too hard to discover ways in which you can serve others. You are only limited by your own creativity. The key is to do something that benefits the other person.

Why is service so important? Because Jesus through His cross served us and expects us to continue His work in the world. To be unwilling to serve others means that you have probably not received the benefits of His service and feel no compulsion to pass it on. Please understand that this does not mean that you are a Jesus follower because you serve, but rather when you are one you do. It is the natural response to God's grace. Once you have it you must give it away.

Challenge: Find someone who needs a service you are capable of providing, and serve them. For some, the home is the perfect place to start. For others, co-workers and neighbors will offer you ample opportunity to serve them.

34
THE WORD

The Bible is a powerful resource. It is the Word of God. Have you ever heard someone say that they don't know what God wants them to do? The best advice is to read the Bible more consistently. They should not only read it, but they need to study it and grow in their understanding. God's Word will guide us if we let it!

"Your word is a lamp to my feet and a light to my path."
Psalm 119:105

When the path is dark and the way is unclear, the Scriptures will give us the direction we need. The longest chapter in the Bible is all about the Bible. It is reliable, and we can follow its instructions without concern; it's always right. What about interpretations you ask? An easy way to know if it is being interpreted correctly is to look at what it meant to the first audience. Scriptural content without cultural context leaves you confused. The Bible will never mean what the Bible never meant. Yes, many have twisted its meaning for their own personal gain. But, that is not the Bible's fault. It is taken out of context far too often.

It can be hard to know what to do when the Bible doesn't specifically speak to your situation. In those cases, it is important to know God's heart and intentions. That comes mainly from getting to know Him through His Word. Without that we can easily go astray. When you are doing your best to do what it says, you trust that you are in the will of God for your life. Then the challenge is simply doing the next right thing. A Jesus follower without a connection to the Word of God is an oxymoron. We should all be growing in our knowledge of Scripture. Without it, we are just making things up.

God can and does speak through people as well, but He will never say anything in conflict with His own Word. Even when you run into two texts that seem at odds, believe them both! The issue is usually our understanding, never the Scripture itself. We are to use the Scriptures to defend against opposing views that would walk us away from God. This is why people memorize Scriptures, to keep themselves encouraged and to help defend against arguments, even ones that come from within. Even Jesus used Bible verses to resist the temptation offered Him from the devil. We need to be people who are in and driven by the Bible.

Challenge: Read all of Psalm 119.

35
GIVE IT TO GOD

Where do you take your struggles, fears, and anxieties? Do you talk to a therapist about it? Do you have friends that you can share your whole heart with? Do you have a spouse or parent with whom you share openly? Some people simply choke it down trying to hold all of their worry in. This either makes them implode, or it all bursts out while they explode in anger. It's all because we don't feel like we have safe places to expose our hearts.

Those who love us can grow tired of our constant and repeated worries. After all, they are only human. Even professionals with whom we pay to listen have to create boundaries to protect themselves emotionally. The good news is, there is always someone who wants to hear from you. When you can't get to a counselor, when your friends grow tired of the same old frustrations, God wants to hear about the things that cause your stress.

"Humble yourselves, therefore, under the mighty hand of God so that at the proper time he may exalt you, casting all your anxieties on him, because he cares for you."
1 Peter 5:6-7

It takes humility to come to God with all of your cares. Why? We are in a society that celebrates independence and self-determination. The sad truth is that there is another side to that fierce independence—the same society considers a person weak when the burdens we carry become too much to bear. But, to lay all pride aside and say that you need God is a good thing! God resists our pride, so this is of course the first step. He takes us as we are and with His power lifts us at the right time. Wow! That is why we can give it all to him. He loves us and He wants all that troubles us to be laid bare, because He is big enough to handle it.

One of the most powerful aspects of this Scripture is who wrote it. Peter was arguably Jesus' best friend. He proclaimed boldly that Jesus was the One who came from God to save the world. He was also the very one who denied Jesus when asked if he knew Him. Peter failed to remain faithful when given the chance to represent his faith in Jesus. Because of this he knew what it was like to carry a burden too heavy and to have the Son of God restore and forgive you. Maybe, he is the perfect person to tell us that no matter the issue, God is big enough to hold all of our problems.

Challenge: Pray, but not the rehearsed prayers that we all have said many times. Give God your greatest burdens, your biggest fears, your ultimate worries. If it helps you, write them down and then say them aloud.

36
FAITH WORKS

Talk is cheap. It literally cost nothing. Our culture gives much credit to the loudest and most insistent voice. So many have so much to say, but how many of them have actions to match their words? What if we took the time to allow those with the strongest opinions to show some evidence of those views working in their own lives? How might our world be different? What if we were more consistent with the link between our words and our practice?

The Bible gives us wisdom for such a contradiction.

"What good is it, my brothers, if someone says he has faith but does not have works? Can that faith save him? If a brother or sister is poorly clothed and lacking in daily food, and one of you says to them, "Go in peace, be warmed and filled," without giving them the things needed for the body, what good¹ is that? So also faith by itself, if it does not have works, is dead. But someone

*will say, "You have faith and I have works." Show me
your faith apart from your works, and I will show you
my faith by my works." James 2:14-18*

What good is it? That is the statement that keeps being asked in this Scripture. Do you want to be known for high ideas alone or for a corresponding action? The actions we take prove what we say we believe. To have faith and have no movement based on that faith causes others to question whether that faith is real. To have works alone causes people to assume that there is a faith attached. When we put these two together, faith and action we show a congruence that simply makes sense.

There are many who refuse to be identified with Jesus followers because their words and works don't match. Jesus was not so inconsistent. He did what He said. That is why very few who have a problem with Jesus, they have a problem with us who say we follow His example. Maybe those around us deserve better. Maybe we can be better? What if we said less and did more?

Challenge: Say less today. Listen to others—really listen. Only give advice when asked directly to do so. Then look for opportunities to lend a helping hand. If you see a need, just help with no expectation of gratitude in response.

37

JOY OVER HAPPINESS

Everyone in our world seems to be seeking happiness at all costs. Happiness is a good thing, but biblical happiness is different from how we see it in our culture. Happiness as the Bible sees it as an enviable position of being blessed by God. It is a more temporary blessing. It is something we all should want and be grateful for when those moments come. Our current culture says happiness is a sense of well-being or contentment and is connected to success, or safety, or luck. It is based on what we have, what we have done, and what just happened to occur, which has little to nothing to do with the Lord. Which means that this is not a scriptural perspective. There is nothing wrong with that sense (which is a feeling), but it is not the spiritual state of being that we find in the Word of God.

The pursuit of temporary happiness becomes a problem when we abandon what we know is true and right. People forsake their marriage vows in the name of their own happiness. If they are currently unhappy, they feel they have every right to go after it in another, not realizing that the emotion will eventually fade like it did before. Parents walk away from children for the same reason. When life becomes too much in its current reality, they decide they have a responsibility to look out for themselves. With this selfish definition it is hard to argue that the happiest people in the world are drug addicts who have just taken the drug of their choice.

You have probably discovered the issue with this world's form of happiness, it can be wildly selfish, and it is a moving target. Most people assume that more financial stability will provide for that emotional need; others think its fame and notoriety. The rich and famous constantly report that a lavish lifestyle and lots of attention are not the solution. Many of them have to fight for more than the shallow pursuits that once drove their success. More is not the answer. So what is, you ask?

Joy! We can move in and out of the earthly emotive senses. Even biblical happiness is not guaranteed, and it can change with a new season. But joy endures!

"May the God of hope fill you with all joy and peace in believing, so that by the power of the Holy Spirit you may abound in hope." Romans 15:13

God gives joy as He gives us hope. Have you ever noticed that joy is usually accompanied by something else? Peace, hope, love, and the usual companions. That alone makes it the superior state of being. Joy also leans towards recognizing God's grace and finding gladness for that. Basically, you can have joy even when things are bad. It is not contingent on temporary emotions or even temporary blessings. Being joyful means, you see what Jesus did on the cross and that is enough! When you have joy, happiness is a bonus not the goal.

Challenge: Take a moment of stillness and silence to think about the grace of God. Consider what Jesus has done on the cross for your sins. Process through the reality that you now belong to God. He wants to fill you today with hope, joy, and peace. Allow for two minutes or more to settle your heart in this truth.

38
BE ANGRY

Anger is wrong, right? No, not necessarily. What we do with our anger can become a problem. Think about all the ways that anger is appropriate. If you see someone who is being abused, enslaved, or oppressed? Those are things that make God angry, so yes, you are allowed to join Him in His anger. For instance, if you witness someone punching a kitten in the face ... Anger! When disrespected or hurt or neglected, you are allowed to feel those emotions. Negative emotions are real and to be expected.

There is a difference between being angry and sinning. Many of us don't know the difference because when we were learning to control our anger there was rarely distinction. Anger, frustration, disappointment, and fear look so much alike to a young person. All those complicated feelings are mashed together in a developing mind. For mature adults, there is a distinct separation between these emotions. There are adults who have never learned how to divide anger and sin, but that should not be the kind of character we want to emulate.

"Be angry and do not sin; do not let the sun go down on your anger, and give no opportunity to the devil."
Ephesians 4:26-27

Be angry, but do it without sinning was the message to the church at Ephesus. The Bible says it is possible, so it must be. Is that a hard concept for you? When we stand for what is right, we embrace a thing called righteous anger. This is where you are totally right and mad. Many people who create not-for-profit organizations do it out of anger over a social ill that they feel is being overlooked—for example, stopping hunger among children because they matter to God. A worthy cause is worthy because it's worth being angry about. That rage can now be channeled to make a difference. But, if someone decides to use their fury to hurt others, to cheat, or to steal, then they have crossed the line into sin. It is what you do with your anger that determines its status as sinful or not.

The larger issue happens when we allow our rage to run away with us without a healthy outlet. Then, we give the devil room and opportunity to ruin our lives. Instead of processing our anger in beneficial ways we give our emotions to the one (the devil) who wants to destroy both us and everything connected to us. That is not usually the goal when we experience rage, but it is what we create when we fail to be angry without sinning.

Challenge: Write down the things that make you furious. Then write ways in which you can healthily deal with both your feelings and the cause of the anger. This may give you direction towards managing your own rage and possibly making the world a better place.

39
GREAT COMMISSION

It is easy to take our eyes off our responsibility to reach the world for Jesus when we are enduring a tough season. We can start to implode and miss the opportunities around us to shine our light in the darkness. Before Jesus ascended into heaven, He left His followers with this challenge.

"And Jesus came and said to them, "All authority in heaven and on earth has been given to me. Go therefore and make disciples of all nations, baptizing them in the name of the Father and of the Son and of the Holy Spirit, teaching them to observe all that I have commanded you. And behold, I am with you always, to the end of the age." Matthew 28:18-20

It's amazing to me that Jesus, in this moment, is entrusting a few guys with the task of telling the world about Him. Can you imagine being one of a very small band of people given the charge to change the world?

Have you ever been given a task that you knew you didn't feel prepared for, and the people who were supposed to help you look just as clueless? That is what these few disciples of Jesus probably felt at that moment.

It's a ridiculous request. We know that Jesus can do it, but for us to try is outrageous. There had to be some deep reasons for them to take on such a large endeavor, and we will look at those. But, just like Jesus commanded the first disciples, God is still expecting His followers to share His message. They were asked to go in light of what they had experienced with Him over time. Yes, they were probably afraid, but that was no excuse to refuse to be a part of His mission. He loved them and welcomed them into a bigger story, so they had to do the same in a loving response.

We are and should be moved by love. God graced us to extend grace to the world. We were graced to be gracious. We love because He loved us. Whether we are going to China, to Rwanda, Korea, or to your own subdivision, we should be ever going because God came for us. So, if you're a career missionary or not, your career should be a mission field that you choose to reach for Jesus.

Yes, you may not feel the greatest. You may be a bit down. You still have a responsibility as a Jesus follower to share your love for Him, even in the hard times. If you have to feel better to tell people about a God who loves you and rescued you in spite of your ups and down, then maybe you have allowed your emotional state to run your life too much. People need to know Jesus in easy seasons and difficult ones. Love others by making disciples even now. He is worth it!

Challenge: Share your faith today. Tell someone about your relationship with Jesus and invite them to come and know Him for themselves.

40

GREAT COMMANDMENT (LOVING OTHERS)

Did you know that God is trying to get people's eyes off of this world and onto Him? And did you know we are a piece of that beautiful process? When we choose to love one another, we display to the world that we belong to Him. We can wrestle with our love for God, but when we know He loves us, it should humble and draw us in. He loved us first. When we get to know Him, we should feel compelled to align with His Word and His desire for us. This idea of love in this scripture speaks of intimacy and closeness:

"And one of them, a lawyer, asked him a question to test him. "Teacher, which is the great commandment in the Law?" And he said to him, "You shall love the Lord your God with all your heart and with all your soul and with all your mind. This is the great and first commandment. And a second is like it: You shall

love your neighbor as yourself. On these two com-
mandments depend all the Law and the Prophets."
Matthew 22:35-40

The problem arises when He asks us to love one another! In race relations, political campaigns, and even in spiritual disagreements in our world, this is a commandment that is so easily overlooked! Jesus didn't let us get away with merely loving God! It's easy to proclaim love for God and do nothing about it. It's hard to see a person who is acting unlovely and to love them in the name of God.

Jesus' reply to this young lawyer was an answer right out of Hebrew teaching! It is called the *Sh'mah*, which is a basic statement of faith that was said twice a day. "Love God and people" is a simple summation. Part of this question was probably to simplify all of the Mosaic laws. The other part was probably to find out the core of Jesus' teaching. This was common in Jesus' day when people would be asked basic spiritual questions to qualify one's theological accuracy.

We see in the commandments that stealing, lying, killing, are all wrong, but we can feel justified in not showing love to one another in certain situations. We use our differences as a reason to ignore this critical scripture. We have to be aware that Jesus did not say that love is an easy action.

This love is Agape love! It's not a fickle, quickly forgotten, easily ignored love. It endures through the worst of situations, it moves beyond disagreements, it is not limited by race and culture. Just as Jesus loved us! He doesn't remove the finished work of the cross from us because we doubt or grow frustrated with Him and our lives. He still endures.

If Jesus displayed that kind of love for us and gave us the command that we should love one another the same way, then we can't deny our calling to love one another. Do you go out of your way at your own expense to show love to other believers? Are you in loving relationships as best as possible with others? When we love one another the way Christ loves us, we show the world that we are His followers. If we can't obey the second commandment, then we probably have not fully embraced the first.

Challenge: Take some time to reach out to someone you have had a hard time loving. It could be a person who has been unresponsive or with whom you had a disagreement. Simply let them know that you appreciate them and are grateful for their lives.

41
REST

～⌇～

Rest is one of those elusive necessities of life that we fight to find and struggle to prioritize. We can run around trying to prove ourselves, taking on tasks that are not our own. Rest comes when we refuse to be something other than who God made us to be! It happens when you say "no" for your own good. We are all sinful, wretched, broken and limited, and to deny that is to be woefully unaware of our own issues. You can't even get over addiction without first admitting that you have a problem. So, rest comes in part by admitting that you are unable to do everything on your own. The power of the Gospel is that Jesus has already done all the critical work.

The Christian faith is the only one where we don't have to try to be good. Our standing with God is not based on our own ability. God Himself did something about our sin issue so we didn't have to. Our good works are not needed to balance the cosmic scales. That means we can REST! We don't have to try to get to heaven. Jesus said, "I have already done the work." When He said, "It is finished," it was FINISHED! We have nothing to prove. When God sees us, He sees Jesus' redeeming blood. So, we can rest. Our only job is to reach out to the hand that is already extended to us! Salvation is not up to us. Jesus saves.

> *"All things have been handed over to me by my Father, and no one knows the Son except the Father, and no one knows the Father except the Son and anyone to whom the Son chooses to reveal him. Come to me, all who labor and are heavy laden, and I will give you rest. Take my yoke upon you, and learn from me, for I am gentle and lowly in heart, and you will find rest for your souls. For my yoke is easy, and my burden is light."*
> *Matthew 11:27-30*

The Father has placed all things in Jesus' hands, so we can rely on Him and what He is saying here. We can come to Jesus and know that He will relieve our burdens. We all can rest in what Jesus has done on our behalf. So, the weight that we carry can be lightened by the One who desires to bear it for us. It's a gift of love that was handed to us. We have to smack the hand away, to not receive this precious gift. It takes some time to learn how to live based on Jesus' instructions. But, He is patient and a dutiful teacher.

Yes, you are supposed to act in response to something you could not earn. Our responsibility is to do our part and trust God with everything that is too big for us. Overall, this is a new way of functioning. Instead of relying on our own abilities and intellect, we simply work hard and trust God with the results. Results no longer depend on us or define our success.

So instead of relying on our power with all the pressure falling on us, work well and rest well. We are responsible for following Jesus. We were invited into a journey with God through Jesus. Now our work is a grateful response to a free gift of God. We get to follow Jesus! We get to be a part of a story that is God sized. We get to do good works in His name that He blesses. We get to move then watch Him move in us beyond our little effort. We get to rest in the finished work of the cross. All our efforts remain in light of the work that He has already done!

Challenge: Take a nap. Make time in your schedule to rest your mind and heart and simply relax. Trust God to do more with that time than you could.

42

KEEP PRAYING

Prayer can be exhausting, especially when the answers seem far away. We can all grow fatigued at delays we seem to get from heaven. Is God absent or blind? Or, does He not care about what we have to endure? Jesus addressed this very issue while teaching the disciples. He taught them in story form, a parable, as an illustration that we all can learn from.

"He said, "In a certain city there was a judge who neither feared God nor respected man. And there was a widow in that city who kept coming to him and saying, 'Give me justice against my adversary.' For a while he refused, but afterward he said to himself, 'Though I neither fear God nor respect man, yet because this widow keeps bothering me, I will give her justice, so that she will not beat me down by her continual coming.'" And the Lord said, "Hear what the unrighteous judge says. And will not God give justice to his elect, who cry to him day and night? Will he delay long over them?" Luke 18:2-7

This widow sought justice and seemed to get none. It's obvious that her cause was good and reasonable. This horrible judge seemed to not care about her issue enough to do anything about it. She eventually wore him down by her persistence. This ultimately gave her the fairness she requested. It was because she refused to quit. This is how we are supposed to be with our prayers.

God hears our cries. He sees our struggles and knows them well. There are two issues we most likely run into. First, is our cause just? Second, have we been persistent in our prayers? Each is tricky to figure out, as we usually see our own perspective as right. But is it? Is our prayer in alignment with the will of God? Yes, if we were God, then we would rule on our own behalf. God's purpose is what He moves to fulfill—not necessarily our desires. His will is what is ultimately best for us, even if we can't see it. A just cause is not determined by our need, but by His will.

When it comes to timing, God measures it differently than we do. We pray once and look for the result. Jesus told us that the Father will not delay long. But what is long for the Everlasting Father? If we pray for weeks, months, or years, is that enough? We don't get to determine that. It can be frustrating to wait on God. But, He will come through in His time, according to His will.

Our responsibility is to not give up. This widow kept asking the judge for justice. We must keep asking God for the things that trouble us.

Challenge: Pray again. Pray about the things that you have grown frustrated about. Choose today to not give up until you get an answer. Some find it helpful to create a prayer list where you can track answers.

43
GENEROSITY GIVES

A re you selfish? The topic of generosity is tough because not many people believe they are indeed selfish, but generosity gives. We think that we want more so that we can give. Biblical generosity doesn't require a lot of money; it requires a generous heart. You don't wait until your financial dreams come true to give. You start when you have little and scale it up over time.

"... Give, and it will be given to you. Good measure, pressed down, shaken together, running over, will be put into your lap. For with the measure you use it will be measured back to you." Luke 6:28

When we give, somehow God in His infinite wisdom records it and takes care of us in return. We are more blessed when we give than when we receive only. This seems so unnatural to so many. Jesus is letting us know that not only do we receive when we give, but we somehow receive more. The more generous you are, the more will be given to you. No one knows exactly how this works, but Jesus said that it happens. If we are selfish, then we will be dealt with selfishly.

When we give to others, we become blessed. It is a good thing to make the lives of others more manageable. There are people who would love the things we take for granted. Giving allows us to pass along blessings. Giving is not only financial; we never use some of our belongings that would benefit someone else greatly. Why not help someone else by giving those things away?

If you do give, could you be more generous? When you do your budget, is there an allowance for the needs of others? Do you have several copies of the same items that go unused or ignored? Do you keep extra cash on hand just to give it to someone less fortunate? These are all opportunities to be generous. When we do that, God makes sure that we receive in return.

Challenge: Give to a person in need or a cause that improves the lives of others.

44

FORGIVING GOD

What do you do when you feel like God has let you down? What do you do if God disappoints you? What do you do when you feel like you need to forgive God? Not that God makes mistakes, or is anything less than perfect, as to need our forgiveness. But, we can be disappointed by His perceived actions or inactions. Life can be difficult, and we can find ourselves wondering where God is when we are struggling. This is when faith gets challenging. How you navigate this experience can determine whether you endure the "dark seasons of the soul."

David knew this feeling. In one of His laments, we get a glimpse into a man after God's heart wrestling with one of these dark moments:

"My God, my God, why have you forsaken me? Why are you so far from saving me, from the words of my groaning? O my God, I cry by day, but you do not

answer, and by night, but I find no rest. Yet you are holy, enthroned on the praises of Israel. In you our fathers trusted; they trusted, and you delivered them. To you they cried and were rescued; in you they trusted and were not put to shame." Psalm 22:1-5

Please, catch the tone. It carries the idea that David had been asking and groaning for a while. It is obvious that this is not merely one rough night or a couple of days. David is frustrated that God is not meeting his expectations. He thought God would have done something by this point. The wait bothered him to the point that he was almost accusing God. Do you know the feeling?

David was at a very low moment, and he didn't feel the nearness of the hand of God. He struggled with both despair and fear. It's clear in his disappointment that this is not only human, but it is biblical. Hopefully, that gives you courage. You are not the only one! You have not failed God if you have moments of doubt and gloom. So many of the Lord's beloved children come to a place of frustration and have walked away from God, because they incorrectly assumed that God would do what they wanted. Believers have struggled to navigate their lack of a job, living single for longer than expected, losing loved ones, or enduring a painful divorce.

David forced his eyes onto God, and he remembered God's goodness in the past. Even in disappointment, David knew that relying on God was the only way. God could still be trusted. David didn't allow his disappointment to distance him from God. David let his struggles draw him closer. The same thing can be true of you also. We must remember that the One to whom we cry is the One who can deliver or grant us peace in the midst of trials.

Challenge: Read Psalm 22 three times today. Try to replace David's disappointments with yours, but be sure to use his conclusions, not your own.

45

GOD WITH ME

We hear the Christmas story every year in December. Not the commercialized version with reindeer, trees, snowmen, and a bearded old man in a red suit, but the arrival of the Christ child. Even in church we overlook Mary's predicament as a pregnant young mother, especially in that day and time. She was a woman and a young one being only about fourteen years old, so she was virtually powerless. She was betrothed, which meant she was legally and financially attached to a man who was to be her husband.

Make no mistake about it: Joseph (her betrothed) was done with her. He didn't believe for a moment that God made her pregnant. He was a good man and didn't want to embarrass her publicly. Joseph most likely had never been in a room alone with her, so he knew he didn't do it. It took a visit from an angel to change his mind.

"But as he considered these things, behold, an angel of the Lord appeared to him in a dream, saying, 'Joseph, son of David, do not fear to take Mary as your wife, for that which is conceived in her is from the Holy Spirit. She will bear a son, and you shall call his name Jesus, for he will save his people from their sins.' All this took place to fulfill what the Lord had spoken by the prophet: 'Behold, the virgin shall conceive and bear a son, and they shall call his name Immanuel' (which means, God with us). When Joseph woke from sleep, he did as the angel of the Lord commanded him: he took his wife, but knew her not until she had given birth to a son. And he called his name Jesus." Matthew 1:20-25

This angel was preparing Joseph for the life he would lead in service to God. He would raise Jesus as his own son. But, he would be able to witness a miracle that he would have heard about his whole life as a young Jewish man. He would see Immanuel being born. This title meant that God would literally be in his midst, and he would have a role to play in his life. He would bear witness to a young virgin bringing God into the world. Although life was taking a major unexpected turn, it would be worth it. God with Him would change everything.

Mary and Joseph were about to embark on a journey that would include hardship, being ostracized and ridiculed. They would be fugitives. Everything in their lives would change. Jesus, our Immanuel, should change everything for us as well! Yes, life may be rough, but

Jesus' arrival as a child in a manger prepared the way for our ultimate rescue, and it still does. Joseph and Mary had the courage to enter a life with Jesus, and we can live that life, too. God with you changes everything about you. You are not alone; Immanuel, God, is with you. You can overcome whatever stands in your way because of Immanuel. God is with you!

Challenge: Every time you grow scared, worried, or unsure today say, God is with me, Immanuel!

46
GOD FIGHTS FOR YOU

O pposition comes! We all have challenges that we
must face. Nehemiah is an example of a godly
leader who did the impossible in the face of opposition. Heartbroken over his hometown's condition, he
went to help rebuild the walls of Jerusalem. He raised
money, rallied people, and did a great deal in a record
amount of time, fifty-two days to be exact. He was an
administrative genius, but it was not easy.

The work of rebuilding the wall of the city of Jerusalem
was necessary. Imagine what your home would look
like without walls. How vulnerable would you feel
to the elements and your enemies? When the work
started, things were going well. Many people were
working right near their home. They divided the work-
load, and progress was happening. But then came the
antagonist! Local tormentors from the surrounding
area began taunting and planning to attack the people
while they worked. Although Nehemiah trusted God's

protection, he was prepared to fight for the success of the work.

"And I said to the nobles and to the officials and to the rest of the people, 'The work is great and widely spread, and we are separated on the wall, far from one another. In the place where you hear the sound of the trumpet, rally to us there. Our God will fight for us.' So we labored at the work, and half of them held the spears from the break of dawn until the stars came out."
Nehemiah 4:19-21

It was scary to hear the voices of their adversaries as they worked. How frightening to know that the enemies see your vulnerability and may be ready to attack at any moment. The one confidence was that God was on his people's side. Nehemiah reminded the people that they were not in the fight alone. God would fight for them. Almighty God, all-powerful God, all-knowing God— He would fight for them! This was not a handful of workers versus a bunch of bad guys. This was a handful of workers and God versus the bad guys. That means that no matter what, Nehemiah was going to win.

When moving forward into what God has for you, you have to expect opposition. Just because God gave Nehemiah a burden didn't mean that it would just happen. He had to work at it and defend it. There may be people you know that will be against you, and some-times even includes family and friends. Then there is the devil! (Yes, you should believe in a real devil. Why?

Because Jesus did.) You can't let the fact that you don't have an easy path deter you. Nothing great happens outside of great opposition!

If we are honest, fear is enough to create despair. The potential of what may happen often looms large. Sometimes our biggest enemy is the one in our own heads! Overwhelming fear can keep you from ever trying anything great. Nehemiah never forgot the God factor! God for us is greater than the whole world against us. God can do what we can't. God holds your future. God has a plan for your life even if the enemy himself stands in your way. God's purpose for us cannot be stopped. God is more powerful than our enemies, more powerful than our doubts! God fights for us!

Challenge: Write down your greatest fears and next to each fear write, "But God fights for me!" It helps to be reminded of this powerful truth.

47
FOLLOW ME

"While walking by the Sea of Galilee, he saw two brothers, Simon (who is called Peter) and Andrew his brother, casting a net into the sea, for they were fishermen. And he said to them, "Follow me, and I will make you fishers of men." Immediately they left their nets and followed him." Matthew 4:18-20

The simple invitation to follow Jesus was astounding. This invitation speaks volumes. To someone reading this today, we might miss the power of being welcomed into the life and ministry of a Rabbi (Teacher). Most of the more intellectual youth of the day had been picked by the leading spiritual voices of the day. The men that Jesus invited were the ones who had been passed over. Four of them were fishermen. One was a hated tax collector who was largely considered to be a traitor in his community.

That simple, *Follow me,* was an affirmation of value and identity. They most likely didn't know what they were facing. They would follow Him for three years and join in His ministry. They watched Him heal the sick, raise the dead, and tell the winds to stand still. His followers would even perform miracles themselves. Most of them would lose their lives in service to their Rabbi. They would ultimately experience Jesus dying on the cross and visiting them after His resurrection. He would go from a teacher to their savior.

The disciples would lay their lives down because they never deserved to be a part of this story. They were already overlooked and ignored, and now they were leaders for this new thing called the church. They would eventually turn the world upside down in service to Jesus. He was worth it, because He saw them when no one else did.

We should be just as grateful. Jesus has welcomed you into His service as well. Jesus asked you to follow Him too. We are invited into a God-sized story. He will take us to places we would not go on our own. But, He will do bigger and better things in our lives than we could do on our own, if we will trust His leadership. The fact that we are not good enough but He wants us, wow! The reality that we don't deserve to be used by God should shock and humble us. It is unhealthy and downright foolish to not be in awe of a God who would use us. God asks you to follow Him, and the best thing you could ever do is go with Him.

Challenge: Tell God YES today, all day. Yes, I will go where you want. Yes, I will speak to who you ask. Yes, I will endure what I must. Yes, I will hope in God. Yes, yes, yes!

48
FIGHTING TEMPTATION

Temptation comes for all of us. No one is exempt. I think it is the trick of our adversary, the devil, to make us feel like we are the only ones who feel the pull of temptation. Maybe we should relax in the truth of our yearnings and face this very familiar challenge head-on. Ever since Adam and Eve sinned in the garden, we have all carried this attraction towards darkness. Even Jesus felt this same pull.

"Then Jesus was led up by the Spirit into the wilderness to be tempted by the devil. And after fasting forty days and forty nights, he was hungry. And the tempter came and said to him, 'If you are the Son of God, command these stones to become loaves of bread.' But he answered, 'It is written, "'Man shall not live by bread alone, but by every word that comes from the mouth of God.'"
Matthew 4:1-4

If Jesus was tempted, then it's not a sin to be tempted. What we do with our temptation can become sin. This is a fundamental misunderstanding of temptation. Temptation is the human desire we have toward the things that break God's heart. This deep-seated desire to do things that go against God's will for our lives is common to everyone. Temptation doesn't make you bad; it makes you human.

We feel bad over the desire. What if we threw a little party every time we overcame it?

We live in a world full of temptation. We must be on guard against it. A foolish person assumes that they can never fall or give in quickly to the allure of sin. You shouldn't want to give in. A fully alive heart for Jesus should desire to do the right thing. The temptation should be counterbalanced with a desire to follow God.

Either the devil or our own wicked desire pulls us toward temptation leading us to sin and death. It is not God who tempts you. God is trying to help us overcome our sin. He is not dangling sin in our faces to see if we fail; that is not the nature of God. If Jesus died so that we would not have to be the property of sin, why would God tempt us with it? We are either tempted by our desires or by the devil, pulling on our desires.

Whether it is you or our enemy, you can feel tempted and make a better choice. Jesus' death on the cross means that we are no longer a slave to our desires. He makes us able to overcome temptation, and even when we fail to conquer it, God forgives us if we ask.

Challenge: Every time you overcome a temptation today, throw a one-minute party for yourself. For instance, if you are tempted to give in to anxiety and fear and you refuse to do so, play a song you enjoy and dance a little in your seat. If later you refuse to over-exaggerate a fact, take a moment to give yourself an applause.

49

FIGHTING GIANTS

D avid is one of the most known and admired figures in the Bible. He is revered for his boldness and intensity. He is also responsible for writing many of the psalms. David was a lover of God outside of the public eye, and when he became a public figure, it was because of what he had cultivated in secret. His greatest battle was fought before the whole army of Israel while he was still a youth. It was his victory over a giant.

David was a young man who was primarily a shepherd and a musician. He was the youngest son and largely overlooked, although he was secretly anointed to be king. The nation was at war with the Philistines, and his father sent him to take supplies to the frontlines where his brothers were enlisted among the soldiers.

When David arrived, he didn't see what he expected. He saw a huge man taunting the people of God. This infuriated David, and he was in awe of how many of the army stood by and ignored the enemy's challenge. He was vocal about his disappointment in the soldiers and his belief that God was bigger than this Philistine. He eventually stood before the King and said he would face the giant one-on-one, representing the entire nation.

Why would David feel so confident that he could beat a giant? Was it because David was anointed king? Saul, the current king, was afraid. So, probably not. David did have some victories under his belt that no one had seen. He had defeated a lion and a bear that tried to steal sheep under his care. But, his assurance came from a much richer place than that. He knew his God! David eventually went into battle with nothing more than a few rocks and a sling.

"And the Philistine moved forward and came near to David, with his shield-bearer in front of him. And when the Philistine looked and saw David, he disdained him, for he was but a youth, ruddy and handsome in appearance. And the Philistine said to David, 'Am I a dog, that you come to me with sticks?' And the Philistine cursed David by his gods. The Philistine said to David, 'Come to me, and I will give your flesh to the birds of the air and to the beasts of the field.' Then David said to the Philistine, 'You come to me with a sword and with a spear and with a javelin, but I come to you in the name of the Lord of hosts, the God of the armies of Israel, whom you have defied. This day the Lord will deliver you into my hand, and I will strike

you down and cut off your head. And I will give the
dead bodies of the host of the Philistines this day to
the birds of the air and to the wild beasts of the earth,
that all the earth may know that there is a God in
Israel, and that all this assembly may know that the
Lord saves not with sword and spear. For the battle
is the Lord's, and he will give you into our hand.'"
1 Samuel 17:41-47

David's confidence came from the Lord. He knew that his God was real, strong, and present. It was not the anointing he received or the predators he had triumphed over. It was his trust in a God who was much bigger than the adversary he was facing. Even people who have never opened the Bible know how this story ends. David's faith that God would cause his efforts to succeed was rewarded. God wins, all the time.

We are supposed to be like David. We have all the promises God has given us in Scripture, and that alone should give us some comfort and courage. All of this should be held alongside the ridiculous notion that God, our Heavenly Father, is on our side. That is why we can go and do anything in His name. We are His people, and He will protect us. You can face your giants because you never fight alone. You can defeat even the most overwhelming odds, not because of your own strength, but because of His.

Challenge: Read 1 Samuel 17 and replace Goliath with whatever opposition you are facing.

50

GRUESOME AND GLORIOUS (THE CROSS)

"He was despised and rejected by men, a man of sorrows and acquainted with grief; and as one from whom men hide their faces He was despised, and we esteemed him not. Surely he has borne our griefs and carried our sorrows; yet we esteemed him stricken, smitten by God, and afflicted. But he was pierced for our transgressions; he was crushed for our iniquities; upon him was the chastisement that brought us peace, and with his wounds we are healed. All we like sheep have gone astray; we have turned—every one—to his own way; and the Lord has laid on him the iniquity of us all."
Isaiah 53:3-6

He (Jesus) bore our griefs, the griefs we should have borne. He was pierced for our transgressions (rebellion from God). He paid the penalty for the things we have done. We did the crime, and He did the time. He was crushed for our iniquities, and we all are guilty. He took the punishment instead of us. God laid on Him our sin so that we didn't have to bear it, because we couldn't. Isaiah said it well: We all like sheep have gone astray.

This scripture tells us what the cross is about. It was written close to 700 years before the advent of Jesus. Long before He arrived, Jesus was destined and determined to die a brutal death on our behalf. The cross was not an accident, not evil winning. It was a planned death that provided us life eternal. We are all marked with the same chronic condition called sin, and Jesus is our healer.

Ever wonder how Jesus did this?

It started after He was taken into custody by the local Jewish officials on false charges. He was ushered to the Father of the High Priest Annas' house where He was questioned illegally. They were so mad that they hit him in his face. Then He was taken to the house of Caiaphas the High Priest and was questioned illegally yet again, while people gave false testimony about Him. He eventually told them that He was in fact the Messiah. They blindfolded him and started slapping him in the face. They made a game out of this.

After they grew weary of this twisted game, Jesus' own people took him to the Roman governor Pontius Pilate to be examined. He in turn sent Jesus to Herod because

Jesus was from his district. Herod's men dressed Jesus in fancy clothes, mocking him and placing a crown of thorns on his head while they beat him. Herod sent Jesus back to Pilate while the Jewish leaders followed the whole way.

To Pilate's credit, he didn't see a need to kill Jesus, but the Jewish leaders incite the crowd to start yelling, "Crucify Him!" Pilate, although a wicked person, knew that Jesus' charges were not deserving of death. Jesus was beaten and whipped mercilessly to the point that He was unrecognizable. Then He was marched to His own execution bearing His own heavy cross, though He was beaten so badly He couldn't carry it the whole way. Ultimately, Jesus was nailed in his wrists and feet, made to put his own weight on His open wounds as He was lifted into the air to hang on a tree.

Jesus did all this because He chose to do it for us. This is God's grace. We couldn't deal with our own sin. It was too big for us to overcome, so He did it for us. He loved us so much that He did what we couldn't. It's grace because we couldn't pay for it. We couldn't earn it. It was a free gift: His life for ours.

This is the one in whom we have placed our hope. Jesus is our hope! He gave us hope. It is His promise that was kept. It is in His name that we pray. He is the one who promised us a hopeful future with Him in heaven. No matter how tough life gets—and it gets tough—Jesus tells us to hold on because the best is yet to come. All we must do is to place our trust and hope in the One who died for us.

Challenge: Live a life filled with hope in Jesus!

About the Author

Damian L. Boyd is a devoted follower of Jesus Christ, passionate communicator, visionary leader, and pastor. For close to three decades, he has reached and developed people both nationally and internationally through conferences, high impact events, leadership gatherings, and everyday ministry. He is a well-known speaker and has supplied people with the principles, tools, and resources to live significant lives for the Glory of God.

Damian committed his life to Christ at the age of 16 after a personal encounter with Jesus. Even with a turbulent childhood of poverty, homelessness, and an absentee father, he realized his amazing potential in Christ and allowed his challenging experiences to be testament to God's love, power, and redemption. He became a revolutionary for Christ and challenged those around him to life passionately for the Lord. His life scripture continues to be the theme of his life and ministry. "You are the salt of the earth...You are the light of the world..." (Matthew 5:13-15).

Damian has invested decades of service in the local church. In 2011, he and his family planted a church in the most statistically challenged community in Atlanta. He believes that the local church is vital for a full life in Christ. Damian and Zarat celebrate more than 21 years of marriage and are raising their son, Damian Jr., a gifted, musical teenager with complex medical needs. He loves his family deeply.

This is Damian's third book. His first two are...

College Impact, Empowering Collegiate Christians for Campus Influence (Paramind Publishing 2009)

In Search of Beautiful, Finding Glimpses of God Around You (Xulon Press 2019)

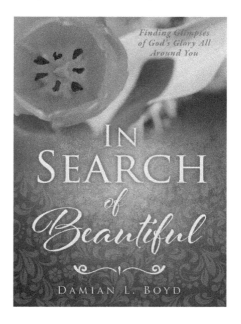

For more information, visit www.damianlboyd.com